The Dark Reality of Banking

Understanding the Creation of Money

Tai-Zamarai Yasharahyalah

The Dark Reality of Banking : Understanding the Creation of Money
Book formatting by Tai-Zamarai Yasharahyalah
Copyright © 2024 by Tai-Zamarai Yasharahyalah
B3 MAGNAT3®

All rights reserved. Printed in the United Kingdom. No part of this book may be used or reproduced in any manner whatsoever without written permission except in the case of brief quotations em- bodied in critical articles or reviews.

Though this book is Non- fiction, Names, characters, businesses, organiza- tions, places, events and incidents are used either as resemblance of real life events and situations or are purely fictitious. Any resemblance to actual persons not intended, living or dead, events, or locales is entirely coincidental.

Instagram, Facebook and YouTube Handle : @B3.FR33

Book and Cover design by Tai-Zamarai Yasharahyalah
©B3 MAGNAT3

First Edition : June 2024

FORWARD

Banking and money creation are cornerstones of our modern economy, yet they remain shrouded in complexity and misunderstanding. The prevalent image of banks merely acting as intermediaries between savers and borrowers is not only oversimplified but also misleading. To fully grasp the impact of banking on our economy, it is crucial to delve into the mechanisms through which banks create money and the broader implications of this process.

Understanding the true nature of banking is not just an academic exercise—it is essential for anyone looking to comprehend the dynamics of economic growth, inflation, and financial stability. The power that banks wield in creating money out of thin air carries significant consequences for our financial system and our daily lives. This book aims to demystify the intricacies of money creation, illuminate the real role of banks, and explore the far-reaching effects on the economy.

In the following chapters, we will dissect how banks generate money, the economic repercussions of their lending practices, and the regulatory challenges that arise. We will also consider potential reforms that could lead to a more stable and equitable financial system. By the end of this journey, readers will have a clearer understanding of how the banking system works and the steps needed to ensure its stability and integrity in the future.

This knowledge is vital for policymakers, financial professionals, and anyone interested in the economic forces that shape our world. It is through this understanding that we can better navigate the complexities of our financial system and work towards a more prosperous and secure economic future.

All You Need to Know About the History of Money, Money Lenders, and Our Current Fractional Reserve Banking System

The evolution of money and banking has been a long journey, marked by significant milestones that have shaped the financial systems we rely on today.

The History of Money:

Money has taken various forms throughout history, from what is now considered 'primitive' barter systems to complex digital currencies. Initially, commodities like gold and silver were used as money due to their intrinsic value and durability. Over time, as trade expanded and economies grew, the need for a more efficient medium of exchange led to the creation of coinage and, eventually, paper money.

Paper money and now digital currencies are simply "I Owe You's," which is supposed to be a receipt showing the gold deposits that the banks are lending from you the depositor—

this is why on any UK paper currency you will see written: pay "the bearer in demand…£5…£10…£20…£50."

Imagine we all went into the banks and demanded our gold deposits?

The Role of Money Lenders: Money lenders have been pivotal in the development of banking. In ancient times, they facilitated trade and commerce by lending money at interest. However, their practices were often viewed with suspicion and were sometimes outlawed due to the high interest rates charged. Despite these challenges, money lending evolved into a more organized banking system.

The Advent of Fractional Reserve Banking:

The concept of fractional reserve banking emerged as banks began to realize that not all depositors would withdraw their money at the same time. This allowed banks to lend out a portion of the deposits while keeping a fraction in reserve. This practice significantly expanded the ability of banks to create money through lending.

Fractional reserve banking works by banks maintaining only a fraction of their depositors' money in reserve and lending out the rest. This system amplifies the money supply through a process called the money multiplier. For example, if the reserve requirement is 10%, a bank can lend out $90 for every $100 deposited, effectively creating new money in the economy.

The Modern Banking System:

Today, our banking system operates on a fractional reserve basis, which has profound implications for money creation and economic stability. Banks create money not by minting coins or printing currency, but by making loans. When a bank issues a loan, it simultaneously creates a deposit in the borrower's account, thereby generating new money.

This process, while essential for economic growth, also carries risks. Excessive lending can lead to inflation and asset bubbles, as seen in various financial crises throughout history. Understanding these dynamics is crucial for managing economic stability and preventing future crises.

Current Challenges and Regulatory Responses:

Modern banking faces numerous challenges, including the need for robust regulatory frameworks to prevent reckless lending and ensure financial stability. Regulatory bodies worldwide strive to balance the benefits of fractional reserve banking with the risks it poses, seeking to protect the economy from potential downturns.

The history of money, the evolution of money lending, and the development of fractional reserve banking are integral to understanding our current financial system. These elements together form the foundation of how banks create money and influence economic activity, highlighting the importance of informed regulation and oversight in maintaining economic stability.

Importance of Understanding the True Nature of Banking for the Economy

In today's complex economic landscape, understanding the true nature of banking is paramount. Banks are not mere intermediaries that facilitate transactions between savers and borrowers; they are powerful institutions that create money and significantly influence economic conditions. Grasping this reality is essential for several reasons:

1. Economic Stability and Growth:

Banks play a crucial role in economic stability and growth through their money creation process. By issuing loans, banks inject new money into the economy, which can stimulate investment, consumption, and overall economic activity. However, if not properly managed, this power can lead to excessive lending, asset bubbles, and financial crises. Understanding how banks operate allows policymakers to craft regulations that promote sustainable economic growth and prevent economic downturns.

2. Inflation Control:

The process of money creation by banks is directly linked to inflation. When banks create too much money through excessive lending, the increased money supply can lead to higher prices for goods and services. Conversely, when lending is restricted, it can lead to deflation. A nuanced understanding of banking practices enables central banks and regulatory authorities to implement monetary policies that maintain price stability, ensuring a balanced and healthy economy.

3. Financial Regulation and Policy:

Effective financial regulation requires a deep understanding of how banks create money and the risks associated with their lending practices. Traditional regulatory frameworks often view banks as intermediaries, which can lead to inadequate oversight. Recognizing banks as money creators highlights the need for more stringent and targeted regulations that address the systemic risks of money creation and lending. This knowledge is crucial for developing policies that protect consumers, ensure the soundness of financial institutions, and prevent economic crises.

4. Risk Management:

Banks' ability to create money comes with significant risks, including the potential for financial instability and systemic crises. Understanding the mechanics of money creation helps in identifying and mitigating these risks. It allows for the development of risk management strategies that can safeguard the financial system against shocks, ensuring a more resilient economy.

5. Consumer Awareness:

Consumers benefit from understanding the true nature of banking, as it impacts their financial decisions and overall economic well-being. Awareness of how banks create money and the implications of their lending practices can lead to more informed decisions regarding savings, investments, and borrowing. This knowledge empowers consumers to make choices that align with their financial goals and helps them navigate the complexities of the financial system.

6. Enhancing Financial Literacy:

A well-informed public is essential for a healthy economy. Financial literacy programs that educate people about the real role of banks and the process of money creation can lead to a more engaged and responsible citizenry. This, in turn, supports a more transparent and accountable financial system.

7. Promoting Fairness and Equity:

Understanding the dynamics of money creation and lending is key to addressing economic inequality. Banks' lending practices can influence the distribution of wealth and opportunities in an economy. By recognizing how money creation can exacerbate or alleviate inequality, policymakers can design interventions that promote fairness and equity, ensuring that the benefits of economic growth are more widely shared.

Understanding the true nature of banking is critical for maintaining economic stability, controlling inflation, crafting effective financial regulations, managing risks, enhancing consumer awareness, promoting financial literacy, and fostering economic equity. This comprehensive understanding is vital for creating a robust and resilient financial system that supports sustainable economic growth and prosperity for all.

Introduction to the Subject of Banking and Money Creation

Banking and money creation are fundamental aspects of our modern financial system, yet they are often misunderstood. At its core, banking is a business that facilitates the flow of money within an economy. Banks accept deposits from individuals and businesses, which they then use to extend loans and create credit. This process of money creation through lending is a critical function that supports economic growth and development.

However, the way banks create money is not straightforward. Contrary to popular belief, banks do not simply lend out deposits they receive. Instead, when a bank grants a loan, it generates new money by creating a corresponding deposit in the borrower's account. This newly created money can then be spent, deposited in other banks, and lent out again, leading to a multiplication of the initial amount of money within the economy.

Central banks, such as the Federal Reserve in the United States or the European Central Bank (ECB) in the Eurozone, play a pivotal role in this system. They oversee the monetary policy, regulate the banking industry, and act as lenders of last resort to ensure financial stability. Central banks also influence money creation by setting interest rates and using various monetary policy tools to control the supply of money.

In recent years, the relationship between central banks and commercial banks has been under scrutiny. The advent of Central Bank Digital Currencies (CBDCs) promises to reshape this dynamic. Unlike traditional money, which is created through bank loans, CBDCs are digital tokens issued directly by central banks. While they offer potential benefits such as enhanced financial inclusion and improved payment efficiency, they also pose significant risks. Central among these risks is the potential for central banks to bypass commercial banks and deal directly with the public, fundamentally altering the structure of the banking system.

Moreover, the programmable nature of CBDCs introduces concerns about privacy and financial control. Central planners could potentially use these digital currencies to track spending, enforce economic policies, or even limit how money is used. This scenario raises important questions about the balance between innovation, financial stability, and individual freedoms.

Understanding the intricate workings of money creation and the evolving role of banks and central banks is essential for navigating the future of finance. This knowledge empowers individuals and policymakers to make informed decisions that can foster economic prosperity and safeguard financial independence.

CONTENT

THE DARK REALITY OF BANKING I

FORWARD 1

CONTENT 9

INTRODUCTION TO THE SUBJECT OF BANKING AND MONEY CREATION 11

PART 1 13

CHAPTER 1 14

A POETIC SYNOPSIS 22

CHAPTER 2 25

CHAPTER 3 40

CHAPTER 4 54

The Dark Reality of Banking: Understanding the Creation of Money

CHAPTER 5 .... **66**

CHAPTER 6 .... **75**

CHAPTER 7 .... **92**

PART 2 .... **117**

CHAPTER 8 .... **118**

CHAPTER 9 .... **138**

CHAPTER 10 .... **151**

CHAPTER 11 .... **162**

CHAPTER 12 .... **176**

CHAPTER 13 .... **190**

CHAPTER 14 .... **206**

SUPPLEMENTARY CHAPTER **225**

STREAMS OF POETRY **255**

ACKNOWLEDGEMENTS **283**

GLOSSARY OF KEY TERMS **287**

ADDITIONAL RESOURCES AND REFERENCES **290**

TAI-ZAMARAI YASHARAHYALAH

Introduction to the Subject of Banking and Money Creation

Banking and money creation are fundamental aspects of our modern financial system, yet they are often misunderstood. At its core, banking is a business that facilitates the flow of money within an economy.

Banks accept deposits from individuals and businesses, which they then use to extend loans and create credit. This process of money creation through lending is a critical function that supports economic growth and development.

However, the way banks create money is not straightforward. Contrary to popular belief, banks do not simply lend out deposits they receive. Instead, when a bank grants a loan, it generates new money by creating a corresponding deposit in the borrower's account. This newly created money can then be spent, deposited in other banks, and lent out again, leading to a multiplication of the initial amount of money within the economy.

Central banks, such as the Federal Reserve in the United States or the European Central Bank (ECB) in the Eurozone, play a pivotal role in this system. They oversee the monetary policy, regulate the banking industry, and act as lenders of

The Dark Reality of Banking: Understanding the Creation of Money

last resort to ensure financial stability. Central banks also influence money creation by setting interest rates and using various monetary policy tools to control the supply of money.

In recent years, the relationship between central banks and commercial banks has been under scrutiny. The advent of Central Bank Digital Currencies (CBDCs) promises to reshape this dynamic. Unlike traditional money, which is created through bank loans, CBDCs are digital tokens issued directly by central banks. While they offer potential benefits such as enhanced financial inclusion and improved payment efficiency, they also pose significant risks. Central among these risks is the potential for central banks to bypass commercial banks and deal directly with the public, fundamentally altering the structure of the banking system.

Moreover, the programmable nature of CBDCs introduces concerns about privacy and financial control. Central planners could potentially use these digital currencies to track spending, enforce economic policies, or even limit how money is used. This scenario raises important questions about the balance between innovation, financial stability, and individual freedoms.

Understanding the intricate workings of money creation and the evolving role of banks and central banks is essential for navigating the future of finance. This knowledge empowers individuals and policymakers to make informed decisions that can foster economic prosperity and safeguard financial independence.

TAI-ZAMARAI YASHARAHYALAH

Part 1

BANKS AND MONEY CREATION

The Dark Reality of Banking:
Understanding the Creation of Money

Chapter 1

The Role of Banks in the Economy

Overview of the Banking System's Function

Banks play a central role in the functioning of modern economies. They are fundamental institutions that facilitate a range of financial activities necessary for economic stability and growth. The primary functions of banks can be summarized as follows:

1. *Financial Intermediation:*

Banks act as intermediaries between savers and borrowers. They collect deposits from individuals and businesses that have surplus funds and lend these funds to those who need capital for various purposes, such as purchasing homes, funding business operations, or financing large projects. This process of financial intermediation helps to allocate resources efficiently across the economy.

2. *Payment and Settlement Systems:*

Banks provide essential payment and settlement services that enable the transfer of funds between parties. This includes everyday transactions like paying bills, purchasing goods and services, and transferring money. These services are crucial for the smooth operation of the economy, ensuring that money can move quickly and securely between parties.

3. *Safekeeping and Custody Services:*

Banks offer safekeeping and custody services for money and valuable items. By providing secure storage and protecting

The Dark Reality of Banking: Understanding the Creation of Money

against theft or loss, banks give depositors peace of mind and confidence in the security of their assets.

4. Credit Creation:

One of the most critical functions of banks is the creation of credit. When banks issue loans, they create new deposits in the banking system, effectively increasing the money supply. This process, known as credit creation, is fundamental to economic expansion. By providing businesses and consumers with access to credit, banks enable investment and consumption that drive economic growth.

5. Risk Management and Diversification:

Banks help manage and diversify financial risks. Through the pooling of deposits and the diversification of loan portfolios, banks can spread risks across a wide range of assets and borrowers. This risk management is essential for maintaining financial stability and protecting both the banks and their customers from potential losses.

6. Facilitating Economic Development:

Banks support economic development by financing infrastructure projects, small businesses, and other economic activities that contribute to national growth. By providing the necessary capital for these projects, banks play a vital role in the development and expansion of the economy.

7. Monetary Policy Implementation:

Central banks rely on commercial banks to implement monetary policy. Through mechanisms such as reserve requirements, open market operations, and interest rate adjustments, central banks influence the amount of money and credit in the economy. Commercial banks are instrumental in this process as they respond to central bank policies by adjusting their lending and deposit-taking activities.

8. *Providing Financial Advice and Services:*

Banks offer a variety of financial services and advice to individuals and businesses. These services include wealth management, investment advice, retirement planning, and insurance products. By helping clients make informed financial decisions, banks contribute to overall economic well-being and financial literacy.

The Importance of Banks in Economic Stability

Banks are not merely passive entities within the economy; they actively shape economic conditions. Their ability to create credit and manage financial risks directly impacts economic stability and growth.
For instance, during periods of economic downturn, banks can help stabilize the economy by continuing to provide credit and maintaining confidence in the financial system.

However, the concentration of power within the banking sector also poses risks. Poor lending practices, excessive risk-taking, and lack of regulation can lead to financial crises, as seen in the 2008 global financial crisis. Thus, while

The Dark Reality of Banking: Understanding the Creation of Money

banks are essential for economic stability and growth, their operations must be carefully monitored and regulated to prevent systemic risks.

In summary, the banking system's functions are multi-faceted and deeply intertwined with the overall health of the economy. Banks facilitate the flow of funds, create credit, manage risks, and support economic development. Understanding these functions is crucial for recognizing the vital role banks play in our economic lives and the importance of maintaining a stable and well-regulated banking system.

Misconception about Banks as Mere Intermediaries

Banks are often perceived as simple intermediaries that take deposits from savers and lend them to borrowers. This conventional view suggests that banks merely pool the savings of depositors and redistribute them in the form of loans. While this image might provide a straightforward understanding of banking, it is a misconception that oversimplifies and misunderstands the true nature of banking operations.

The Traditional View

In the traditional view, banks are seen as financial intermediaries:

1. *Deposits and Loans*: Customers deposit their money into banks, which then hold these deposits and lend them out to other customers.

2. *Interest Spread*: Banks earn profits by charging borrowers a higher interest rate on loans than they pay to depositors on their savings.

3. *Liquidity Management*: Banks manage the liquidity needs of their customers, ensuring that depositors can withdraw their funds on demand while keeping enough reserves to meet these withdrawals.

The Reality: Banks as Money Creators

However, the reality of modern banking goes beyond mere intermediation:

1. *Creation of Money*: Banks have the unique ability to create money through the lending process. When a bank issues a loan, it does not transfer existing money from one account to another. Instead, it generates new money by

The Dark Reality of Banking: Understanding the Creation of Money

crediting the borrower's account with a deposit, which did not exist before the loan was made.

2. *Balance Sheet Expansion*: This process expands the bank's balance sheet, with the loan appearing as an asset and the new deposit as a liability.

3. *Fractional Reserve Banking*: Banks operate under a fractional reserve system, meaning they are only required to keep a fraction of their deposits as reserves. This enables them to lend out multiples of their actual reserves, further amplifying their money-creating capacity.

Misunderstanding the Function of Banks

The misconception of banks as mere intermediaries leads to several misunderstandings:

1. *Impact on Money Supply*: Viewing banks solely as intermediaries underestimates their influence on the money supply. The money creation process means that banks play a direct role in the expansion and contraction of the economy's overall money supply.

2. *Regulatory Implications*: Misunderstanding the true function of banks can lead to inadequate regulatory frameworks. Effective regulation must account for banks' ability to create money and the associated risks.

3. *Economic Stability*: Recognizing banks' role as money creators highlights their importance in maintaining economic stability. Unchecked money creation can lead to asset bubbles and financial crises, emphasizing the need for prudent lending practices and robust oversight.

The Importance of Accurate Understanding

1. *Policy Making*: Accurate understanding of the banking system is crucial for policymakers to design effective economic policies and regulations that ensure financial stability and sustainable growth.

2. *Public Awareness*: Educating the public about the true nature of banking helps consumers make informed decisions about their financial activities and encourages greater accountability from financial institutions.

3. *Innovation and Reform*: A clear understanding of banking functions can drive innovation and reform in the financial sector, fostering a more resilient and transparent banking system.

Banks are far more than mere intermediaries. They are powerful creators of money, and their operations significantly impact the economy. Recognizing this reality is essential for developing a robust and stable financial system that supports sustainable economic growth.

The Dark Reality of Banking: Understanding the Creation of Money

A Poetic Synopsis

"The Guardians Gold."

In vaults of glass and digital streams,

Where gold and cryptic tokens gleam,

There lies a power, vast and grand,

In banks that shape our common land.

No longer mere custodians old,

Of silver bars and coins of gold,

They craft new wealth from air unseen,

Through loans and debts in markets keen.

A dance of credits, debts, and trade,

In ledgers deep, their roles displayed,

Not just as keepers of our pay,

But creators of the cash we lay.

TAI-ZAMARAI YASHARAHYALAH

In times of need, their vaults unlock,

To lend, to build, to share, to stock,

They fuel the dreams of those who dare,

To innovate, to grow, to care.

But with this power comes a weight,

To steer clear of a risky fate,

For when they falter, nations fall,

Their echoes ring through market halls.

So heed the lessons of the past,

In balances and checks held fast,

For banks, with all their might and means,

Are keystones in our fiscal scenes?

To millennials, both bold and new,

Who seek to shape a future true,

Understand this banking lore,

For in its depths, your fortunes soar.

The Dark Reality of Banking: Understanding the Creation of Money

Embrace the knowledge, wield it well,

And in this world, your dreams compel,

To craft a future bright and free,

With wisdom from this treasury.

Chapter 2

Banks as Money Creators

Explanation of How Banks Create Money Out of Thin Air

The concept of banks creating money out of thin air might sound surprising or even implausible, yet it is a fundamental aspect of modern banking systems. Unlike the simplistic view that banks merely redistribute existing money from savers to borrowers, banks actually generate new money through the lending process.

The Process of Money Creation

1. **Loan Issuance**: When a bank approves a loan, it does not transfer money from its existing deposits. Instead, it credits the borrower's account with a deposit equivalent to the loan amount. This new deposit is created from nothing—hence the phrase "money out of thin air."

2. **Balance Sheet Mechanics**:

- *Asset Creation*: The loan appears as an asset on the bank's balance sheet because it represents a future stream of payments from the borrower.

- *Liability Creation*: Simultaneously, the newly created deposit appears as a liability because the bank now owes this amount to the borrower.

3. *Fractional Reserve System*: Banks operate under a fractional reserve system, meaning they are required to keep

only a fraction of their depositors' money in reserve. This fraction is determined by regulatory requirements, such as the reserve ratio set by central banks. The remaining funds can be lent out, enabling the creation of additional money.

An Example of Money Creation

To illustrate, consider a scenario where a customer, Alice, takes out a £10,000 loan from her bank:

1. *Deposit Creation*: The bank credits Alice's account with £10,000. Alice now has £10,000 in her account that she can use immediately.

2. *Loan as an Asset*: This £10,000 loan is recorded as an asset on the bank's balance sheet.

3. *Deposit as a Liability*: Concurrently, the £10,000 in Alice's account is a liability for the bank, as it represents money the bank owes to Alice.

4. *Reserve Requirements*: If the reserve requirement is 10%, the bank needs to hold only £1,000 in reserve against Alice's £10,000 deposit. The remaining £9,000 can potentially be used to make more loans, further creating money.

The Multiplier Effect

This money creation process leads to a multiplier effect:

1. *Subsequent Deposits and Loans*: When Alice spends her £10,000, the recipient of this money deposits it into their bank. This bank can then lend out a significant portion of this deposit, repeating the process of money creation.

The Dark Reality of Banking: Understanding the Creation of Money

2. *Expansion of Money Supply*: Each round of lending and deposit creation expands the money supply. The total amount of money created depends on the reserve ratio and the willingness of banks and borrowers to engage in additional loans.

Regulatory and Economic Implications

Understanding the money creation process has significant implications:

1. *Monetary Policy*: Central banks, such as the Federal Reserve or the Bank of England, influence money creation primarily through setting reserve requirements and interest rates. By adjusting these levers, they can control the amount of money banks create, impacting inflation, economic growth, and overall financial stability.

2. *Risk Management*: Excessive money creation can lead to asset bubbles and financial instability. Prudent regulation and oversight are necessary to ensure that banks lend responsibly and that money creation aligns with productive economic activities.

3. *Public Perception*: Misconceptions about money creation can lead to misunderstandings about the nature of economic policies and the role of banks in the economy. Educating the public about how banks create money can foster a more informed and engaged populace.

Conclusion

Banks play a pivotal role in the economy by creating money through the lending process. This money creation is not merely a redistribution of existing funds but the generation of new money that fuels economic activity. Recognizing and understanding this process is essential for developing effective monetary policies, maintaining financial stability, and fostering a well-informed public.

Emperical Evidence Suporting This View

The notion that banks create money out of thin air is not merely a theoretical concept; it is supported by substantial empirical evidence. Various studies, central bank reports, and academic research have demonstrated and explained this phenomenon in detail.

Central Bank Statements and Studies

1. *Bank of England Reports*

- In 2014, the Bank of England published a seminal report titled "Money Creation in the Modern Economy," which explicitly stated that "commercial banks create money, in the form of bank deposits, by making new loans." The report

The Dark Reality of Banking: Understanding the Creation of Money

clarified that the common perception of banks as intermediaries between savers and borrowers is outdated and incorrect.

- The report further explained that when a bank makes a loan, it simultaneously creates a matching deposit in the borrower's bank account, thereby creating new money.

2. *Deutsche Bundesbank*:

- Germany's central bank, Deutsche Bundesbank, has also acknowledged the money creation role of banks. It stated that "the majority of the money supply is created by private banks granting loans."

- The Bundesbank emphasized that bank loans create deposits, which are new money, rather than simply transferring existing funds.

Academic Research

1. *Werner's Studies:*

- Economist Richard A. Werner conducted a detailed empirical study published in 2014, where he demonstrated that banks do not simply intermediate between savers and borrowers but create new money when they issue loans.

- In his study, Werner observed the lending practices of a small bank and found that the bank did not reduce its reserves or liquidate assets to issue a loan. Instead, it created a new deposit in the borrower's account, illustrating money creation.

2. *McLeay, Radia, and Thomas (Bank of England)*

- In their 2014 paper, "Money Creation in the Modern Economy," McLeay, Radia, and Thomas provided detailed evidence of how commercial banks create money. They used balance sheet mechanics and real-world examples to show that bank loans result in new deposits and, consequently, new money in the economy.

Real-World Examples

1. *Post-2008 Financial Crisis:*

- The 2008 financial crisis highlighted the role of banks in money creation and its impact on the economy. During the crisis, the significant reduction in bank lending led to a contraction in the money supply, exacerbating the economic downturn.

- Central banks around the world, including the Federal Reserve and the European Central Bank, responded by implementing unconventional monetary policies such as Quantitative Easing (QE) to inject liquidity into the banking system. These measures were aimed at encouraging banks to lend and thus create new money to stimulate economic recovery.

2. *Quantitative Easing (QE):*

- QE is a process where central banks purchase financial assets, such as government bonds, from commercial banks and other financial institutions. This increases the reserves of these banks, enabling them to create more loans and, consequently, more money.

- Studies on the effectiveness of QE have shown that it can significantly expand the money supply and influence economic activity. For instance, research by the Bank of Japan demonstrated that QE policies helped increase the money supply and mitigate deflationary pressures in the Japanese economy.

Statistical Evidence

1. *Money Supply Data:*

- Analysis of money supply data (M1, M2, M3) often reveals that the majority of money in circulation is created by commercial banks rather than central banks. For instance, in the UK and the US, a significant portion of the money supply is in the form of bank deposits, which are created through the lending activities of commercial banks.

- Historical data show that periods of increased bank lending correspond with expansions in the money supply, while periods of reduced lending correspond with contractions.

2. *Credit Growth and Economic Activity*:

- Empirical studies have found a strong correlation between credit growth (bank lending) and economic activity. For example, a study by the International Monetary Fund (IMF) found that rapid credit growth often precedes economic booms, while sharp contractions in credit growth are associated with economic recessions.

- This correlation underscores the critical role of banks in creating money and influencing economic cycles.

Conclusion

Empirical evidence from central bank reports, academic research, real-world examples, and statistical data robustly supports the view that banks create money out of thin air. Understanding this process is crucial for policymakers, economists, and the public, as it has profound implications for monetary policy, financial regulation, and economic stability. Recognizing the true nature of banking as a money-creating mechanism allows for more informed decisions that can enhance economic resilience and growth.

Legal Definitions and Implications of Deposits and Loans

Understanding the legal definitions and implications of deposits and loans is essential to grasp how banks create money. The legal framework governing banking transactions clarifies the nature of these financial activities and their impact on money creation.

Legal Definitions

1. **Deposits:**

- *Legal Status*: In legal terms, a bank deposit is not a bailment (where property is placed in the custody of another) or a trust. Instead, it is a loan from the depositor to the bank. When you deposit money in a bank, you are essentially lending that money to the bank.

The Dark Reality of Banking:
Understanding the Creation of Money

- *Ownership*: Upon deposit, the money becomes the bank's property, and the depositor gains a claim against the bank for the amount deposited. This claim is reflected as a liability on the bank's balance sheet.

2. **Loans**:

- *Loan Agreement*: A loan is a contractual agreement where a bank extends credit to a borrower with the obligation of repayment with interest. The borrower receives funds (or the equivalent credit), which they agree to repay over a specified period.

- *Asset Creation*: When a bank grants a loan, it creates an asset on its balance sheet (the loan itself) and a corresponding liability (the deposit credited to the borrower's account).

Implications for Money Creation

1. **Balance Sheet Mechanics**:

- *Loan Issuance*: When a bank issues a loan, it simultaneously creates a deposit in the borrower's account. This deposit is new money, created out of thin air, and increases the money supply.

- *Double-Entry Bookkeeping*: The bank's balance sheet records the loan as an asset and the new deposit as a liability. This double-entry bookkeeping is fundamental to understanding how money is created.

2. **Fractional Reserve Banking**:

- *Reserves and Lending*: In a fractional reserve banking system, banks are required to hold only a fraction of their deposits as reserves. This means they can lend out the majority of the deposits, thereby creating more money through the issuance of new loans.

- *Money Multiplier Effect*: The process of repeatedly issuing loans and creating deposits leads to a multiplication of money in the economy. For example, with a reserve requirement of 10%, a deposit of £1,000 can theoretically support up to £10,000 in new loans and deposits.

3. **Legal Implications**:

- *Deposit Insurance*: Legal frameworks often include deposit insurance schemes to protect depositors in case of bank failure. This insurance enhances trust in the banking system, encouraging more deposits and thereby facilitating further money creation.

- *Regulatory Oversight*: Laws and regulations govern the extent and manner in which banks can create money. These include reserve requirements, capital adequacy standards, and lending restrictions aimed at ensuring financial stability.

4. **Economic Implications**:

- *Monetary Policy*: Central banks influence money creation through monetary policy tools such as reserve requirements, interest rates, and open market operations. By adjusting these tools, central banks can indirectly control the amount of money that banks create.

- *Credit Allocation*: The legal framework affects how credit is allocated in the economy. Regulations can steer lending towards productive uses, such as business investment, rather than speculative activities, thereby impacting economic growth and stability.

The Dark Reality of Banking: Understanding the Creation of Money

Case Studies and Examples

1. **Historical Examples**:

- *Great Depression*: During the Great Depression, the failure of banks led to a contraction in the money supply, illustrating the critical role of bank-created money in economic stability. The legal responses included the establishment of the FDIC (Federal Deposit Insurance Corporation) in the United States to restore trust and encourage deposits.

- *2008 Financial Crisis*: The 2008 crisis highlighted the risks associated with excessive money creation through unproductive lending. Legal reforms, such as the Dodd-Frank Act in the US, aimed to enhance regulatory oversight and prevent future crises.

2. **Modern Examples**:

- *Quantitative Easing (QE):* Post-2008, central banks implemented QE, which involved large-scale asset purchases to increase bank reserves. This policy aimed to encourage banks to lend more, thus creating more money and stimulating economic activity.

- *Negative Interest Rates*: In some jurisdictions, central banks have implemented negative interest rates to incentivize banks to lend rather than hold excess reserves, further illustrating the legal and economic interplay in money creation.

Conclusion

The legal definitions and implications of deposits and loans are foundational to understanding how banks create money. By recognizing that deposits are loans to banks and that loans result in new deposits, we can appreciate the mechanisms behind money creation. This understanding is crucial for effective monetary policy, regulatory frameworks, and maintaining economic stability. Through legal structures and regulations, we can guide the process of money creation to support sustainable economic growth and prevent financial crises.

A Poetic Synopsis

"Illusions of Wealth."

Out of thin air, banks conjure gold,

In vaults of trust, their secrets hold.

With ink and ledgers, wealth they spin,

A magician's trick, where does it begin?

Empirical truths unravel the lore,

Deposits and loans, the heart of the core.

☐

The Dark Reality of Banking: Understanding the Creation of Money

Not mere keepers of coin and bill,

But creators of wealth, at their own will.

Loans transform, deposits arise,

New money flows as old myths die.

A borrower's note, a promise sealed,

In banking's game, the truth revealed.

Legal words, their meanings deep,

In vaults of power, quietly creep.

Deposits as loans, the cycle spins,

In this alchemy, each act begins.

Economies rise on promises made,

In this dance of debt, fortunes are laid.

Banks as creators, wielders of might,

Turning whispers of credit into the light.

Thus, in shadows of vaults so grand,

Banks sculpt the future, lending hand.

TAI-ZAMARAI YASHARAHYALAH

A force unseen, yet felt by all,

In this dance of money, we rise, we fall.

Chapter 3

The Mechanics of Money Creation

Detailed Breakdown of How Banks Record Debts and Create Deposits

Understanding the mechanics of money creation requires delving into the detailed processes by which banks record debts and create deposits. These processes hinge on the principles of double-entry bookkeeping and the fractional reserve banking system.

The Process of Recording Debts and Creating Deposits

1. Double-Entry Bookkeeping:

- *Basic Principle*: Double-entry bookkeeping requires that for every financial transaction, there are two corresponding entries: a debit and a credit. This system ensures that the accounting equation (Assets = Liabilities + Equity) remains balanced.

- *Example*: When a bank grants a loan, it records a credit entry under "Loans Receivable" (an asset) and a debit entry under "Deposits" (a liability).

The Dark Reality of Banking: Understanding the Creation of Money

2. Loan Issuance:

- **Step-by-Step Process:**

1. *Loan Agreement*: The bank and borrower enter into a loan agreement specifying the amount, interest rate, repayment schedule, and other terms.

2. *Creation of Loan*: The bank creates a loan on its balance sheet. For example, if the loan amount is £10,000, the bank records a £10,000 loan receivable (asset).

3. *Deposit Creation*: Simultaneously, the bank credits the borrower's account with a £10,000 deposit (liability). This deposit represents new money that the borrower can now use.

- **Implications**: The creation of a loan increases the bank's assets (the loan receivable) and liabilities (the deposit). The money supply in the economy increases by the amount of the loan.

3. Fractional Reserve Banking:

- *Reserve Requirements*: Banks are required to hold a fraction of their deposits as reserves, either in cash or as deposits with the central bank. This requirement ensures liquidity and stability in the banking system.

- *Lending Capacity*: With a reserve requirement of 10%, a bank that receives a £10,000 deposit must hold £1,000 in reserve but can lend out £9,000. This process can be repeated as the newly created deposits are re-deposited into the banking system.

4. Money Multiplier Effect:

- *Initial Deposit*: Consider an initial deposit of £10,000 in Bank A.

- *Lending Process*: Bank A lends out £9,000 (keeping £1,000 in reserve). The £9,000 is then deposited in Bank B, which holds £900 in reserve and lends out £8,100, and so on.

- *Cumulative Effect*: The initial deposit of £10,000 can lead to a total increase in the money supply of up to £100,000, assuming a 10% reserve requirement.

Example Scenario

Loan Creation:

- *Bank and Borrower Agreement*: John approaches Bank X for a £20,000 personal loan.

- *Bank Records Loan*: Bank X records a £20,000 loan receivable on its balance sheet.

- *Deposit Creation*: Simultaneously, John's account is credited with a £20,000 deposit.

Fractional Reserve Banking:

- *Reserve Requirement*: Bank X is required to hold 10% of John's deposit as reserves, i.e., £2,000.

- *Remaining Amount*: Bank X can lend out the remaining £18,000.

The Dark Reality of Banking: Understanding the Creation of Money

- *Money Multiplier*: If the £18,000 is deposited into another bank and the process continues, the initial £20,000 loan could lead to a substantial increase in the total money supply.

Implications for the Economy

1. Economic Growth:

- *Investment and Spending*: The newly created money from loans stimulates economic activity by funding investments and consumption.

- *Multiplier Effect*: The money multiplier effect amplifies the impact of initial lending, potentially leading to significant economic growth.

2. Inflation:

- *Demand-Pull Inflation*: If the money supply grows faster than the economy's capacity to produce goods and services, it can lead to demand-pull inflation, where too much money chases too few goods.

- *Monetary Policy*: Central banks monitor money creation to control inflation by adjusting interest rates and reserve requirements.

3. Financial Stability:

- *Credit Risk*: Excessive lending, particularly to unproductive sectors, can lead to defaults and financial instability.

- *Regulatory Oversight*: Regulatory frameworks aim to ensure that banks maintain sufficient reserves and engage in prudent lending practices to mitigate risks.

Conclusion

The mechanics of money creation through the recording of debts and creation of deposits are central to the functioning of modern banking. By understanding the detailed processes and their implications, we can better appreciate the role of banks in economic growth, inflation control, and financial stability. This knowledge underscores the importance of effective regulatory oversight and prudent banking practices in maintaining a healthy economy.

The Process of Purchasing Promissory Notes and its Implications

The processes of purchasing promissory notes is a cornerstone of how banks create money. When a borrower approaches a bank for a loan, the bank assesses the borrower's creditworthiness and, if satisfied, agrees to lend the money. This transaction involves the borrower signing a promissory note, which is a written promise to repay the loan amount with interest over a specified period.

How Promissory Notes Work

1. *Creation of Debt*: When the borrower signs the promissory note, they are essentially creating a debt. The

The Dark Reality of Banking: Understanding the Creation of Money

note specifies the principal amount, interest rate, repayment schedule, and other terms of the loan.

2. *Bank's Balance Sheet*: Upon accepting the promissory note, the bank records it as an asset on its balance sheet because it represents future income from interest and principal repayments. Simultaneously, the bank creates a corresponding deposit in the borrower's account, which is recorded as a liability because the bank owes this amount to the borrower.

3. *Money Creation*: This act of recording the promissory note and creating a deposit effectively generates new money. The bank did not transfer existing funds to the borrower; instead, it created new money in the form of a deposit, which the borrower can use immediately.

Implications of Promissory Note Transactions

1. *Increased Money Supply*: Each loan issued by a bank increases the money supply within the economy. This process underpins the modern monetary system where money is predominantly created through lending activities by commercial banks rather than by printing physical currency.

2. *Economic Activity*: The newly created money can stimulate economic activity as borrowers use the funds for various purposes such as purchasing goods, investing in businesses, or paying for services. This can lead to economic growth if the borrowed money is used productively.

3. *Debt Dependency*: The economy becomes increasingly dependent on debt. As more money is created through loans,

the overall debt levels in the economy rise. This can lead to potential risks, especially if borrowers default on their loans or if the economy slows down, making it difficult to repay the debts.

4. *Interest Payments*: Since banks earn interest on the loans they issue, the repayment of loans with interest can lead to a transfer of wealth from borrowers to banks. This creates a continuous cycle where new loans are needed to service existing debts, perpetuating the creation of new money.

5. *Monetary Policy Influence*: Central banks influence the money creation process through monetary policy tools like interest rates and reserve requirements. By adjusting these parameters, central banks can indirectly control the amount of money banks create, thus managing economic stability and inflation.

6. *Regulatory Considerations*: The process of money creation through lending necessitates stringent regulatory oversight to ensure financial stability. Regulators monitor banks' lending practices, capital adequacy, and risk management strategies to prevent excessive risk-taking and ensure the soundness of the financial system.

Understanding the process of purchasing promissory notes and its implications provides insight into the critical role banks play in money creation and the broader economic impacts of their lending activities. This knowledge is essential for comprehending how modern economies function and the inherent risks and benefits of a debt-driven financial system.

Proposed Solutions

Addressing the implications of how banks create money through the purchase of promissory notes and ensuring the stability of the financial system requires a multifaceted approach. Below are some proposed solutions:

Strengthening Regulatory Frameworks

1. *Enhanced Capital Requirements*: Increasing the minimum capital reserves that banks must hold can help absorb potential losses and reduce the risk of insolvency. This makes the banking system more resilient to economic shocks.

2. *Stricter Lending Standards*: Implementing rigorous criteria for loan approval can ensure that credit is extended only to creditworthy borrowers and for productive purposes. This reduces the likelihood of defaults and speculative lending.

3. *Regular Stress Testing*: Conducting frequent stress tests on banks to evaluate their ability to withstand adverse economic conditions can help identify vulnerabilities and prompt corrective actions before crises occur.

4. *Improved Transparency*: Mandating greater transparency in banks' operations, including detailed disclosures about their lending practices and risk exposures, can enhance

accountability and enable better monitoring by regulators and the public.

Promoting Responsible Lending

1. *Credit Allocation Policies*: Encouraging or mandating banks to direct a higher proportion of their lending towards productive sectors, such as small businesses and infrastructure projects, can foster sustainable economic growth.

2. *Limits on Speculative Lending*: Imposing caps on the amount of lending that banks can allocate to speculative investments, such as real estate and financial markets, can help prevent asset bubbles and financial instability.

3. *Consumer Protection Measures*: Strengthening consumer protection laws to prevent predatory lending practices can safeguard borrowers and promote fair lending practices.

Central Bank Interventions

1. *Macroprudential Policies*: Central banks can implement macroprudential measures, such as countercyclical capital buffers and loan-to-value ratio limits, to manage systemic risks and smooth out the credit cycle.

2. *Quantitative Easing Adjustments*: Adjusting the scope and scale of quantitative easing programs can influence the amount of money banks create. Central banks can tailor these programs to support specific economic objectives, such as reducing unemployment or stimulating investment in green technologies.

The Dark Reality of Banking: Understanding the Creation of Money

Encouraging Alternative Banking Models

1. *Support for Community Banks*: Providing incentives for the establishment and growth of community banks, which are more likely to lend to local businesses and projects, can diversify the banking landscape and promote more equitable economic development.

2. *Public Banking Options*: Establishing public banks that operate with a mandate to serve public interests rather than profit maximization can provide a stable source of funding for essential services and infrastructure.

3. *Cooperative Banking*: Encouraging cooperative banking models, where banks are owned and governed by their members, can align banking practices with the needs of the community and promote responsible lending.

Financial Education and Awareness

1. *Public Education Campaigns*: Launching comprehensive financial literacy programs to educate the public about how banks create money and the implications of borrowing can empower individuals to make informed financial decisions.

2. *Transparency in Banking Operations*: Promoting transparency in how banks operate and how they create money can help demystify the banking system and build public trust.

Technological Innovations

1. *Blockchain and Digital Currencies*: Exploring the use of blockchain technology and central bank digital currencies (CBDCs) can offer more transparent and secure alternatives to traditional banking practices, potentially reducing the reliance on bank-created money.

2. *Fintech Solutions*: Leveraging financial technology (fintech) to provide more efficient and accessible financial services can increase competition and innovation in the banking sector, leading to better outcomes for consumers and businesses.

By implementing these solutions, policymakers and financial institutions can address the challenges associated with the current money creation process and work towards a more stable, transparent, and equitable financial system.

A Poetic Synopsis

"Alchemy of Ledgers."

In vaults unseen, the alchemy starts,

Banks weave new wealth from ledgered charts.

A promissory note, a pledge to repay,

Transforms to deposits by the break of day.

☐

The Dark Reality of Banking: Understanding the Creation of Money

No gold exchanged, no coins in hand,

Just numbers shifted by a digital band.

A loan granted, a debt incurred,

From thin air, wealth conferred.

The borrower signs, the banker nods,

A dance of balance sheets, no need for gods.

Debt recorded, money appears,

A conjured currency, fueling fears.

Promissory notes, promises made,

Ink on paper, fortunes weighed.

Yet this creation, fraught with risk,

Demands vigilance, not a gambler's frisk.

Regulations must be firm and tight,

To guide this alchemy towards the light.

For in the balance of debts and dues,

Lies the power to shape our economic muse.

TAI-ZAMARAI YASHARAHYALAH

So, understand this subtle art,

Banks as magicians, playing their part.

In the creation of money, the stakes are high,

Guardians of the vaults, under the watchful sky.

Chapter 4

Economic Impacts of Bank-Created Money

How Money Creation Aligns with Economic Productivity

The process of money creation by banks has profound implications for economic productivity. When banks issue new loans, they generate new money, which can stimulate various sectors of the economy, potentially leading to growth and development. Here's how this alignment occurs:

1. *Investment in Business Ventures*:

- Banks provide capital to entrepreneurs and businesses, enabling them to invest in new projects, expand operations, and innovate. This investment can lead to increased production, job creation, and technological advancements, all of which contribute to economic growth.

2. *Infrastructure Development*:

- Loans for infrastructure projects, such as roads, bridges, and public facilities, can enhance economic efficiency by reducing transportation costs, improving access to markets, and facilitating trade. These projects often have a multiplier effect, stimulating additional economic activities and employment.

3. *Housing and Real Estate:*

- Mortgage loans allow individuals to purchase homes, which drives demand in the housing market. This demand, in turn, spurs construction activities, creating jobs and stimulating related industries such as manufacturing and retail.

4. *Consumer Spending:*

- Personal loans and credit lines enable consumers to purchase goods and services, driving demand in the economy. Increased consumer spending can boost retail sales, support businesses, and encourage further investment.

5. *Agricultural and Rural Development:*

- Access to credit can empower farmers and rural businesses to invest in better equipment, seeds, and technology, leading to higher agricultural productivity and improved living standards in rural areas.

6. *Education and Skills Development:*

- Loans for education can enhance human capital by enabling individuals to acquire new skills and knowledge. A more educated and skilled workforce can improve productivity and innovation, benefiting the overall economy.

7. *Research and Development (R&D):*

- Financing for R&D can lead to breakthroughs in science and technology, fostering innovation and competitiveness. These advancements can open up new markets, improve efficiency, and create high-value jobs.

Balancing Productivity and Inflation

While the alignment of money creation with economic productivity can drive growth, it is crucial to balance this process to avoid inflation. If the supply of money grows faster than the economy's capacity to produce goods and services, it can lead to price increases, reducing the purchasing power of money. Therefore, effective monetary policy and regulation are essential to ensure that money creation supports sustainable and stable economic growth.

The Relationship Between Money Creation, Inflation and Economic Stability

The interplay between money creation, inflation, and economic stability is a delicate balance that is crucial for a healthy economy. Here's a detailed look at how these elements interact:

1. Money Creation and Inflation:

- *Mechanism:* When banks create money by issuing loans, the overall money supply in the economy increases. If this increase in money supply outpaces economic growth, where the production of goods and services does not keep up, it can lead to inflation. Inflation occurs because more money chases the same amount of goods, pushing up prices.

The Dark Reality of Banking:
Understanding the Creation of Money

- *Demand-Pull Inflation*: Excessive money creation can lead to demand-pull inflation, where increased demand from higher spending outstrips supply, leading to price rises.

- *Cost-Push Inflation*: While not directly tied to money creation, cost-push inflation occurs when the costs of production increase (e.g., due to higher wages or raw material costs), which can be exacerbated by excessive money in circulation if it leads to higher wages and costs.

2. Economic Stability:

- *Stimulation of Growth*: When used wisely, money creation can stimulate economic growth by providing the necessary capital for businesses to invest in new projects, hire more employees, and innovate. This growth can lead to higher output and productivity.

- *Risks of Overexpansion*: However, if banks create too much money without corresponding growth in economic output, it can lead to economic instability. This instability often manifests in the form of asset bubbles, where prices of assets such as real estate or stocks increase rapidly and unsustainably. When these bubbles burst, they can lead to severe economic downturns and financial crises.

- *Credit Booms and Busts*: Excessive credit growth can lead to boom-and-bust cycles. During a boom, easy credit fuels rapid growth and speculative investments. When the bust comes, it can result in widespread defaults, banking crises, and recessions.

3. Managing Inflation and Stability:

- *Monetary Policy*: Central banks play a critical role in managing the balance between money creation and economic stability. By adjusting interest rates and using other monetary policy tools, central banks can influence the amount of money in circulation. For instance, higher interest rates can reduce borrowing and money creation, helping to control inflation.

- *Regulatory Measures*: Effective regulation of the banking sector is essential to prevent excessive risk-taking and ensure that money creation supports productive investments rather than speculative bubbles. Regulations can include capital requirements, lending standards, and oversight mechanisms.

- *Inflation Targeting*: Many central banks adopt an inflation-targeting framework, aiming for a specific inflation rate to maintain price stability. This approach helps anchor inflation expectations and provides a clear guideline for monetary policy.

4. Case Studies and Historical Examples:

- *Hyperinflation*: Historical instances of hyperinflation, such as in Zimbabwe or Weimar Germany, illustrate the dangers of uncontrolled money creation. In these cases, excessive printing of money led to runaway inflation, eroding the value of currency and causing severe economic disruption.

- *Moderate Inflation*: On the other hand, moderate inflation, typically around 2-3%, is often considered beneficial. It encourages spending and investment rather than hoarding money, supporting ongoing economic activity and growth.

While bank-created money can drive economic growth, it must be carefully managed to prevent inflation and ensure long-term economic stability. Balancing money supply with economic output, maintaining prudent lending practices, and implementing effective regulatory frameworks are key to achieving this balance.

Proposed Solutions

To mitigate the risks associated with bank-created money and ensure economic stability, a multifaceted approach involving regulatory reforms, monetary policy adjustments, and structural changes in the banking sector is essential. Here are some proposed solutions:

1. Stronger Regulatory Oversight:

- *Enhanced Capital Requirements*: Banks should maintain higher capital reserves to absorb potential losses and reduce the risk of insolvency during economic downturns.

- *Leverage Limits*: Imposing stricter leverage limits can prevent banks from taking on excessive debt relative to their equity, thus curbing speculative lending practices.

- *Loan-to-Value Ratios*: Setting maximum loan-to-value (LTV) ratios for different types of loans can help prevent asset bubbles, particularly in real estate markets.

2. Prudent Monetary Policy:

- *Interest Rate Adjustments*: Central banks should use interest rate policies proactively to manage economic cycles, raising rates to curb excessive borrowing and lowering them to stimulate growth during downturns.

- *Quantitative Easing and Tightening*: These tools can help manage the money supply directly. Quantitative easing can inject liquidity into the economy during crises, while quantitative tightening can withdraw excess money during boom periods.

- *Inflation Targeting*: Central banks should continue to adopt and refine inflation-targeting frameworks to maintain price stability and anchor inflation expectations.

3. Macroprudential Measures:

- *Systemic Risk Monitoring*: Establishing institutions to monitor and address systemic risks in the financial sector can preemptively identify and mitigate emerging threats.

- *Stress Testing*: Regular stress testing of banks can ensure they have adequate capital buffers to withstand economic shocks.

- *Counter-Cyclical Capital Buffers*: Implementing counter-cyclical capital buffers that increase during boom periods and decrease during recessions can help stabilize the financial system.

4. Promoting Sustainable Lending:

- *Credit Allocation Policies*: Encouraging or mandating that a certain proportion of bank lending goes towards productive investments (e.g., SMEs, infrastructure projects) rather than speculative activities.

- *Community Banking*: Supporting the growth of community banks and credit unions that focus on local, productive lending can foster economic resilience and reduce the concentration of financial power.

5. Financial Education and Transparency:

- *Public Awareness Campaigns*: Increasing public understanding of how banking and money creation work can lead to more informed decision-making and pressure for better regulatory practices.

- *Transparency Requirements*: Requiring banks to disclose detailed information about their lending practices and risk exposures can enhance market discipline and regulatory oversight.

6. International Cooperation:

- *Global Regulatory Standards*: Harmonizing regulatory standards across countries can prevent regulatory arbitrage, where banks move operations to less regulated jurisdictions.

- *Coordination of Monetary Policies*: Greater coordination among central banks can help manage global liquidity and address transnational financial risks.

7. Technological Innovations:

- *Fintech Integration*: Leveraging financial technology (fintech) to improve risk assessment, enhance transparency, and provide alternative lending platforms can contribute to a more resilient financial system.

- *Digital Currencies*: Exploring the implementation of central bank digital currencies (CBDCs) could provide a more direct tool for monetary policy and reduce reliance on private bank-created money.

Implementing these proposed solutions requires a coordinated effort between regulators, central banks, financial institutions, and the public. By strengthening regulatory frameworks, adopting prudent monetary policies, promoting sustainable lending, enhancing transparency, fostering financial education, encouraging international cooperation, and leveraging technological innovations, we can create a more stable and resilient banking system. This, in turn, will help align money creation with economic productivity, control inflation, and ensure long-term economic stability.

A Poetic Synopsis

"Whispers of Wealth: The Mechanics of Creation."

In halls where whispers craft unseen,

Banks spin their threads in a quiet sheen.

With pens as wands, they conjure gold,

In ledgers deep, the tales unfold.

Not mere vaults of coin and note,

But creators where numbers float.

From thin air, deposits rise,

The Dark Reality of Banking: Understanding the Creation of Money

Promissory notes, the banker's prize.

A loan, they say, is just a start,

A pledge, a bond, a promise part.

Yet in the script of debts and dues,

New money births, with silent cues.

The promissory notes they buy,

In ledgers firm, the figures fly.

Deposits swell, unseen, unheard,

A magician's spell in every word.

Yet magic here is wrought with care,

For every coin they must prepare.

The balance holds, a delicate weave,

Between what's lent and what's received.

Thus, in the vaults of modern lore,

Banks create and lend much more.

A cycle spun from naught to might,

TAI-ZAMARAI YASHARAHYALAH

In the shadows, in the light.

Economies rise on this creation,

Yet caution needs a firm foundation.

For every loan and every line,

Echoes through the hands of time.

In whispers deep and figures grand,

Banks shape the wealth across the land.

But let us see with eyes anew,

The power in the hands of few.

Thus, understand this tale so old,

Of how banks' secrets turn to gold.

In knowing, guard the future's way,

Where money's magic holds its sway.

...

Chapter 5

The Risks of Unproductive Lending

Consequences of Banks Focusing on Speculative Lending

In the world of finance, banks hold the power to shape economies through their lending practices. While productive lending can spur economic growth and stability, unproductive or speculative lending poses significant risks. When banks focus excessively on speculative investments, the consequences can be dire and far-reaching.

Asset Bubbles: Speculative lending often fuels asset bubbles, where the prices of assets such as real estate, stocks, or commodities are driven far above their intrinsic value. This occurs when banks extend credit to borrowers who invest in these assets, leading to inflated prices. As more money chases the same assets, prices continue to rise, creating an unsustainable bubble.

Economic Inequality: Speculative lending can exacerbate economic inequality. Wealthier individuals and entities typically have better access to credit and are more likely to engage in speculative investments. As asset prices rise, those who own these assets see their wealth increase, while those without such investments are left behind, widening the wealth gap.

Financial Instability: Asset bubbles are inherently unstable.

The Dark Reality of Banking: Understanding the Creation of Money

When the bubble bursts, asset prices plummet, leading to significant financial losses for investors. Banks that have extended large amounts of credit for speculative purposes may face substantial losses, which can lead to a banking crisis. The resulting financial instability can ripple through the economy, affecting businesses, employment, and overall economic growth.

Misallocation of Resources: When banks prioritize speculative lending over productive lending, resources are diverted from sectors that contribute to economic growth and development. Instead of funding businesses that create jobs and produce goods and services, credit is funneled into speculative ventures that do not add real value to the economy.

Increased Debt Levels: Speculative lending often leads to increased debt levels among borrowers. When the value of speculative investments falls, borrowers may find themselves unable to repay their loans. This can lead to defaults and bankruptcies, further destabilizing the financial system.

Moral Hazard: Speculative lending can create moral hazard, where borrowers and lenders engage in risky behavior because they do not bear the full consequences of their actions. If banks believe they will be bailed out by the government in the event of a crisis, they may be more inclined to take excessive risks.

The focus on speculative lending undermines the fundamental role of banks as facilitators of economic growth. To mitigate these risks, it is essential to implement robust regulatory frameworks that encourage productive lending and discourage speculative practices. By aligning banking practices with the broader goals of economic stability and growth, we can create a more resilient financial system.

Case Studies of Asset Bubbles and Financial Crises

Examining historical case studies of asset bubbles and financial crises provides valuable insights into the consequences of unproductive lending. These events illustrate the dangers of speculative investments and the profound impact they can have on economies.

1. The Great Depression (1929-1939):

The stock market crash of 1929 marked the beginning of the Great Depression, a period of severe economic downturn in the United States and worldwide. In the 1920s, banks extended significant credit for stock market speculation. As stock prices soared, many investors borrowed heavily to purchase stocks, believing prices would continue to rise indefinitely. When the market crashed in October 1929, it triggered a cascade of bank failures and bankruptcies. The ensuing economic collapse led to widespread unemployment, poverty, and a contraction in global trade. The Great Depression highlighted the catastrophic impact of speculative lending and underscored the need for regulatory reforms to stabilize the financial system.

2. The Japanese Asset Price Bubble (1986-1991):

In the late 1980s, Japan experienced a massive asset price bubble, driven by speculative lending in real estate and stock

The Dark Reality of Banking:
Understanding the Creation of Money

markets. During this period, Japanese banks provided extensive loans to real estate developers and investors, fueling a sharp rise in property and stock prices. By the early 1990s, the bubble burst, leading to a dramatic decline in asset values. The collapse severely impacted the Japanese economy, resulting in a prolonged period of economic stagnation known as the "Lost Decade." The banking sector was burdened with non-performing loans, leading to bank failures and a crisis of confidence in the financial system. This case study illustrates the long-term economic damage that can result from speculative lending practices.

3. The Dot-Com Bubble (1995-2000):

The dot-com bubble was characterized by a rapid rise in the valuations of internet-based companies during the late 1990s. Venture capitalists and banks invested heavily in technology startups, often without regard for their profitability or long-term viability. Stock prices of tech companies soared, driven by speculative trading. By 2000, the bubble burst, leading to a sharp decline in the stock market and significant financial losses. Many tech companies went bankrupt, and the broader economy experienced a slowdown. This crisis highlighted the risks of speculative investment in emerging industries and the importance of due diligence in lending and investing.

4. The Global Financial Crisis (2007-2008):

The global financial crisis was one of the most severe economic downturns since the Great Depression, triggered by the collapse of the housing market in the United States. In the years leading up to the crisis, banks engaged in extensive speculative lending through subprime mortgages. These high-risk loans were often bundled into mortgage-backed securities and sold to investors. When housing prices began to fall, mortgage defaults soared, leading to massive losses for financial institutions. The crisis resulted in the failure of major banks, a severe credit crunch, and a global recession. The aftermath saw significant government interventions and reforms aimed at preventing future crises, emphasizing the need for prudent lending practices and robust financial regulation.

5. The European Sovereign Debt Crisis (2010-2012):

The European sovereign debt crisis primarily affected countries in the Eurozone, such as Greece, Ireland, Portugal, Spain, and Italy. The crisis was fueled by excessive borrowing and speculative investments in government bonds. Banks and investors, attracted by high yields, lent large sums to these countries, leading to unsustainable debt levels. When concerns about debt repayment grew, bond yields soared, and several countries faced the threat of default. The crisis led to severe austerity measures, economic contractions, and social unrest in the affected nations. It underscored the interconnectedness of global financial systems and the dangers of speculative lending to sovereign entities.

These case studies demonstrate the significant risks associated with unproductive lending and speculative investments. They highlight the importance of sound regulatory frameworks and prudent lending practices to ensure financial stability and sustainable economic growth. By learning from these historical examples, policymakers and financial institutions can better navigate the challenges of modern financial markets.

The Dark Reality of Banking: Understanding the Creation of Money

A Poetic Synopsis

"Shadows of Unproductive Lending."

In vaults of dreams and paper gold,

Where fortunes rise and stories fold,

Banks, in shadows, cast their spell,

Yet tales of ruin they oft foretell.

Great Depression's haunting call,

A market soared, then watched it fall.

Loans to gamble, hopes were dashed,

A world in sorrow, fortunes crashed.

Japan's bubble, real estate high,

Mountains of money, touching the sky.

But dreams can burst, like bubbles do,

Leaving a decade lost, in economic rue.

TAI-ZAMARAI YASHARAHYALAH

Dot-Com era, tech dreams bold,

Investments wild, stories sold.

A burst of pixels, fortunes turned,

A lesson in fire, where many burned.

Crisis global, housing's plight,

Mortgages spun, in greed's delight.

When homes collapsed, a market bled,

Global whispers of panic spread.

Europe's sovereign debt in flight,

Loans to nations, in reckless sight.

Austerity's grip, economies froze,

A cautionary tale, of lending woes.

In each of these, the lesson clear,

Banks' creations, instilled in fear.

Speculative whispers, markets swell,

Yet shadows loom, where fortunes fell.

Guard the vaults, with wisdom's key,

The Dark Reality of Banking: Understanding the Creation of Money

Prudent lending, the path must be.

For in the echoes of bubbles past,

Lies the wisdom, to ensure we last.

Chapter 6

Regulatory Challenges and Solutions

Current Regulatory Shortcomings

The current regulatory framework for banking and finance is fraught with significant shortcomings that fail to adequately address the complexities and risks inherent in the modern financial system. Here are some of the most pressing issues:

1. *Outdated Perspectives:*

- Many regulations are based on the traditional view of banks as mere intermediaries rather than as creators of money. This outdated perspective leads to insufficient oversight of the money creation process.

2. *Fragmented Oversight:*

- Regulatory oversight is often fragmented among multiple agencies, leading to gaps and overlaps in supervision. This fragmentation can result in critical areas being neglected and regulatory arbitrage by financial institutions.

3. *Inadequate Stress Testing:*

- Stress tests conducted by regulators often fail to accurately predict the resilience of banks in extreme economic scenarios. The assumptions used in these tests can be overly optimistic, leading to a false sense of security.

4. *Capital Requirements:*

- Current capital requirements may not be stringent enough to cover the potential losses from high-risk lending activities. This inadequacy can leave banks vulnerable to financial shocks and contribute to systemic risk.

5. *Shadow Banking:*

- The rise of shadow banking – financial activities conducted by non-bank institutions – often escapes regulatory scrutiny. This sector can pose significant risks to financial stability due to its lack of transparency and regulatory oversight.

6. *Complex Financial Products:*

- The proliferation of complex financial products, such as derivatives, poses challenges for regulators. These instruments can be difficult to value and manage, increasing the risk of market instability.

7. *Global Coordination:*

- Inadequate global coordination among regulators can lead to regulatory gaps and inconsistencies. Financial markets are global, but regulation is often national, leading to challenges in managing cross-border financial risks.

8. *Incentive Structures:*

- Incentive structures within banks, such as bonuses tied to short-term performance, can encourage excessive risk-taking. These structures often prioritize short-term gains over long-term stability.

9. *Regulatory Capture:*

- Regulatory agencies may be susceptible to capture by the industries they are supposed to regulate. This can result in

The Dark Reality of Banking: Understanding the Creation of Money

regulations that favor industry interests over public interest and financial stability.

10. *Technological Advancements:*

- Rapid advancements in financial technology (FinTech) can outpace regulatory frameworks, creating new risks that are not adequately addressed by existing regulations. This includes cybersecurity threats and the rise of cryptocurrencies.

Proposed Solutions

1. *Adopt a Modern View of Banking:*

- Regulations should reflect the modern understanding of banks as creators of money. This includes closer scrutiny of the money creation process and ensuring that it aligns with economic stability.

2. *Streamline Regulatory Agencies:*

- Consolidate regulatory oversight to reduce fragmentation and improve coordination. A more streamlined regulatory framework can enhance the effectiveness of supervision and reduce the risk of regulatory arbitrage.

3. *Enhance Stress Testing:*

- Improve the realism and robustness of stress tests by incorporating more severe and varied economic scenarios. This will provide a better assessment of banks' resilience to financial shocks.

4. *Strengthen Capital Requirements:*

- Increase capital requirements to ensure that banks have sufficient buffers to absorb losses from high-risk lending activities. This can help mitigate systemic risk and enhance financial stability.

5. *Regulate Shadow Banking:*

- Extend regulatory oversight to include shadow banking activities. This involves improving transparency and applying appropriate regulations to non-bank financial institutions to mitigate risks.

6. *Simplify Financial Products:*

- Encourage the use of simpler financial products and improve the transparency and valuation of complex instruments. This can help reduce market instability and enhance regulatory oversight.

7. *Improve Global Coordination:*

- Enhance international cooperation and coordination among regulators to address cross-border financial risks. This includes sharing information and harmonizing regulatory standards.

8. *Revise Incentive Structures:*

The Dark Reality of Banking: Understanding the Creation of Money

- Reform incentive structures within banks to align with long-term stability rather than short-term performance. This can help reduce excessive risk-taking and promote sustainable banking practices.

9. *Mitigate Regulatory Capture:*

- Implement measures to prevent regulatory capture, such as stricter conflict-of-interest policies and increased transparency. This can ensure that regulations serve the public interest and financial stability.

10. *Address Technological Risks:*

- Update regulatory frameworks to keep pace with technological advancements in FinTech. This includes addressing cybersecurity threats, regulating cryptocurrencies, and ensuring that new technologies do not undermine financial stability.

Historical Examples of Effective Banking Regulation

Effective banking regulation has played a crucial role in maintaining financial stability and preventing crises. Here are some notable historical examples:

1. The Glass-Steagall Act (1933)

The Glass-Steagall Act, officially known as the Banking Act of 1933, was enacted in the United States in response to the Great Depression. This legislation introduced several key reforms:

- *Separation of Commercial and Investment Banking*: The Act prohibited commercial banks from engaging in investment banking activities, thereby reducing the risk of speculative investments with depositors' funds.

- *Creation of the FDIC*: The Federal Deposit Insurance Corporation (FDIC) was established to provide insurance for bank deposits, which helped restore public confidence in the banking system.

The Glass-Steagall Act effectively stabilized the banking sector by reducing conflicts of interest and ensuring that banks focused on their core functions. Although parts of the Act were repealed in 1999, its principles remain influential in discussions about banking regulation.

2. Basel Accords

The Basel Accords are a series of international banking regulations developed by the Basel Committee on Banking Supervision (BCBS), which provides recommendations on banking laws and regulations:

- *Basel I (1988):* Established minimum capital requirements for banks to reduce credit risk. It introduced the concept of risk-weighted assets, ensuring that banks held capital proportional to their risk exposure.

- *Basel II (2004):* Enhanced the framework of Basel I by introducing three pillars: minimum capital requirements, supervisory review, and market discipline. It aimed to improve risk management and transparency.

- *Basel III (2010):* Developed in response to the 2008 financial crisis, Basel III introduced stricter capital requirements, leverage ratios, and liquidity standards to improve the resilience of banks in times of financial stress.

The Basel Accords have significantly influenced global banking practices by promoting sound risk management and enhancing the stability of the international financial system.

3. The Dodd-Frank Act (2010)

The Dodd-Frank Wall Street Reform and Consumer Protection Act was enacted in the United States following the 2008 financial crisis. Key provisions include:

- *Consumer Financial Protection Bureau (CFPB):* Established to protect consumers from abusive financial practices and to enforce consumer financial laws.

- *Volcker Rule*: Prohibited banks from engaging in proprietary trading and limited their investments in hedge funds and private equity funds to reduce risky activities.

- *Enhanced Oversight*: Increased regulatory oversight of financial institutions, particularly those deemed "too big to fail," and introduced stress testing to assess their resilience to economic shocks.

The Dodd-Frank Act aimed to prevent another financial crisis by addressing the systemic risks and regulatory gaps exposed by the 2008 meltdown.

4. Canada's Banking System

Canada's banking system is often cited as one of the most stable and well-regulated in the world. Key features include:

- *Conservative Lending Practices*: Canadian banks are known for their conservative lending practices and stringent mortgage regulations, which have contributed to financial stability.

- *Strong Regulatory Framework*: The Office of the Superintendent of Financial Institutions (OSFI) oversees the banking sector and enforces strict capital and liquidity requirements.

- *Limited Exposure to Subprime Mortgages:* During the 2008 financial crisis, Canadian banks had limited exposure to subprime mortgages, which helped them weather the global financial turmoil.

Canada's regulatory approach, characterized by prudence and strong oversight, has been effective in maintaining a resilient banking sector.

5. Post-War Japanese Banking Regulation

After World War II, Japan implemented a series of banking reforms that contributed to its economic recovery and growth:

The Dark Reality of Banking: Understanding the Creation of Money

- *Government-Led Industrial Policy*: The Japanese government, through the Ministry of Finance and the Bank of Japan, directed credit to strategic industries, fostering rapid industrialization and economic development.

- *Keiretsu System*: The close relationships between banks and industrial corporations (keiretsu) facilitated access to credit and investment, driving economic growth.

While this model eventually faced challenges, particularly during the asset bubble of the late 1980s, it played a crucial role in Japan's post-war economic miracle.

Conclusion

These historical examples demonstrate the importance of effective banking regulation in ensuring financial stability and preventing crises. Each example highlights different regulatory approaches tailored to specific economic contexts and challenges. Understanding these precedents can inform contemporary efforts to enhance banking regulation and promote a resilient financial system.

Proposal for New Regulatory Frameworks

To address the contemporary challenges in the banking sector and prevent future financial crises, several proposals for new regulatory frameworks have been put forward. These proposals aim to enhance the stability, transparency, and accountability of the banking system. Here are some key proposals:

1. Stricter Capital Requirements

- *Increased Capital Buffers*: Banks should maintain higher capital reserves to absorb potential losses during economic downturns. This includes raising the minimum capital adequacy ratios beyond those stipulated by Basel III.

- *Countercyclical Capital Buffers*: Implement capital buffers that vary with the economic cycle, requiring banks to build up capital in good times that can be drawn down during periods of stress.

2. Enhanced Liquidity Requirements

- *Liquidity Coverage Ratio (LCR):* Strengthen the LCR to ensure that banks hold sufficient high-quality liquid assets to withstand short-term liquidity disruptions.

- *Net Stable Funding Ratio (NSFR):* Ensure that banks maintain a stable funding profile in relation to the composition of their assets and off-balance sheet activities.

3. Leverage Ratio Caps

- *Tighten Leverage Ratios*: Introduce more stringent leverage ratio requirements to limit the extent to which banks can leverage their equity capital, thereby reducing the risk of insolvency.

4. Comprehensive Stress Testing

- *Regular and Rigorous Stress Tests*: Conduct frequent and rigorous stress tests to evaluate banks' resilience to various economic scenarios, including severe recessions and market shocks.

- *Transparency in Stress Testing*: Ensure that the results of stress tests are publicly disclosed to enhance market discipline and provide stakeholders with a clear understanding of banks' risk profiles.

5. Stronger Regulation of Systemically Important Financial Institutions (SIFIs)

- *Higher Standards for SIFIs*: Impose stricter regulatory standards on SIFIs, including higher capital and liquidity requirements, to mitigate the risks they pose to the broader financial system.

- *Living Wills*: Require SIFIs to create detailed resolution plans, or "living wills," that outline how they can be safely dismantled in the event of failure without causing systemic disruption.

6. Reinstating the Separation of Commercial and Investment Banking

- *Reviving Glass-Steagall Principles*: Consider reinstating the separation of commercial and investment banking activities to reduce conflicts of interest and limit the risks associated with speculative trading.

- *Prohibition of Proprietary Trading*: Implement rules similar to the Volcker Rule, which restricts banks from engaging in proprietary trading and limits their ownership stakes in hedge funds and private equity funds.

7. Strengthening Consumer Protection

- *Robust Consumer Financial Protection*: Enhance the powers and resources of consumer protection agencies to ensure that financial products and services are safe, transparent, and fairly marketed.

- *Financial Literacy Programs*: Invest in financial education initiatives to improve consumers' understanding of financial products and their ability to make informed decisions.

8. Enhanced Oversight and Accountability

- *Improved Governance Standards*: Mandate higher standards of corporate governance within banks, including stricter requirements for board composition, risk management practices, and executive compensation.

- *Whistleblower Protections*: Strengthen protections for whistleblowers who expose malpractices within financial institutions to encourage greater accountability and transparency.

9. Technological and Cybersecurity Regulations

- *Cybersecurity Standards*: Implement stringent cybersecurity standards to protect banks and their customers from cyber threats and ensure the integrity of financial systems.

- *Regulation of Fintech*: Develop a regulatory framework for financial technology (fintech) companies to ensure they operate safely and soundly while promoting innovation.

10. International Coordination

- *Global Regulatory Harmonization*: Promote international coordination and harmonization of banking regulations to prevent regulatory arbitrage and ensure a level playing field for banks operating across borders.

- *Crisis Management Protocols*: Establish clear protocols for managing cross-border financial crises, including mechanisms for cooperation among national regulators and central banks.

Conclusion

These proposals aim to create a more robust and resilient banking system capable of withstanding economic shocks and protecting consumers. By implementing stricter capital and liquidity requirements, enhancing regulatory oversight, and promoting transparency and accountability, we can mitigate the risks inherent in the banking sector and foster a stable and sustainable financial environment.

TAI-ZAMARAI YASHARAHYALAH

A Poetic Synopsis

"Regulation's Redemption."

In halls where money's whispers reign,

Where fortunes rise, and fall like rain,

A call for wisdom, strong and clear,

To guard against the tides of fear.

Banks once unshackled, wild and free,

Now bound by rules for you and me,

Stricter capitals to brace the blow,

When winds of crisis start to blow.

Liquidity like life's own breath,

Must flow unblocked, must fend off death,

Buffers built in times of grace,

To steel us in the darkened place.

Leverage capped, no more excess,

The Dark Reality of Banking: Understanding the Creation of Money

To keep our future free from stress,

Tests of stress to gauge the strain,

Ensuring we can stand the pain.

For giants deemed too big to fail,

We write their end, a careful tale,

Their weight no longer threats our dreams,

With living wills, we change the themes.

A wall between the old and new,

Commercial calm from trades' brew,

Revive the laws of Glass-Steagall's pen,

To bring a safer world again.

Protections for the common folk,

To shield them from the lender's yoke,

With literacy to light their way,

Empowering choices, every day.

Governance with eyes unblind,

TAI-ZAMARAI YASHARAHYALAH

Whistleblowers' voices kind,

In cyber realms and fintech's rise,

Regulations sharpened, wise.

And in this world of global ties,

We harmonize, we synchronize,

A symphony of guarded trade,

Where crisis plans are deftly laid.

Thus, we shape a future bright,

With rules that guard both day and night,

A banking world, both just and fair,

For every dreamer's hopeful stare.

Chapter 7

The Future of Banking and Money Creation

Potential Reforms and Their Impacts

As the financial landscape evolves, the need for reforms in banking and money creation becomes increasingly apparent. Addressing the limitations and risks inherent in the current system can pave the way for a more stable and equitable economy. Here, we explore several potential reforms and their anticipated impacts on the financial sector and broader economy.

1. Central Bank Digital Currencies (CBDCs)

Reform: Introduction of Central Bank Digital Currencies (CBDCs) as an official digital form of currency issued and regulated by the central bank.

Impacts:

- *Increased Financial Inclusion*: CBDCs can provide access to banking services for unbanked populations, promoting financial inclusion and reducing inequality.

- *Enhanced Monetary Policy Transmission*: Direct control over digital currency can improve the effectiveness of monetary policy, allowing central banks to respond more precisely to economic fluctuations.

- *Reduced Costs and Fraud*: Digital currencies can lower transaction costs and reduce fraud by eliminating the need for physical cash.

2. Full Reserve Banking

Reform: Transition to a full reserve banking system where banks are required to hold 100% reserves against their deposits, eliminating the practice of fractional reserve banking.

Impacts:

- *Increased Financial Stability*: Full reserve banking would significantly reduce the risk of bank runs and financial crises, as banks would always have sufficient reserves to meet withdrawal demands.

- *Reduced Money Supply Volatility*: With banks no longer creating money through lending, the money supply would become more stable, potentially reducing inflationary pressures.

- *Challenges for Credit Availability*: This reform could limit the amount of credit available to the economy, potentially slowing economic growth unless alternative credit mechanisms are developed.

3. Narrow Banking

Reform: Implementation of narrow banking, where banks are restricted to holding safe, liquid assets and are prohibited from engaging in risky lending or investment activities.

Impacts:

- *Enhanced Safety of Deposits*: Depositors' funds would be safeguarded, as narrow banks would only invest in low-risk assets, reducing the likelihood of bank failures.

- *Increased Focus on Core Banking Services*: Banks could focus on providing essential banking services, improving efficiency and customer service.

- *Need for Alternative Credit Providers*: With banks limited to safe investments, other institutions might need to fill the gap in providing credit to businesses and consumers.

4. Decentralized Finance (DeFi) Integration

Reform: Integration of decentralized finance (DeFi) platforms into the mainstream financial system, leveraging blockchain technology to facilitate financial transactions.

Impacts:

- *Enhanced Transparency*: Blockchain technology can increase transparency in financial transactions, reducing fraud and improving trust in the financial system.

- *Lower Costs*: DeFi can reduce transaction costs by eliminating intermediaries, making financial services more affordable.

- *Regulatory Challenges*: The integration of DeFi poses regulatory challenges, requiring new frameworks to ensure security and compliance while fostering innovation.

5. Green Banking Initiatives

Reform: Encouragement of green banking practices, where banks prioritize environmentally sustainable projects and investments.

Impacts:

- *Promotion of Sustainable Development*: Green banking can channel funds into sustainable projects, supporting the transition to a low-carbon economy.

- *Reputation and Risk Management*: Banks adopting green practices can enhance their reputation and manage risks associated with climate change.

- *Potential for Higher Costs*: Initial investments in green projects may involve higher costs, which could impact short-term profitability.

6. Strengthening Community Banks

Reform: Support for the growth and development of small, community-oriented banks that focus on local lending and investment.

Impacts:

- *Boost to Local Economies*: Community banks can drive local economic growth by providing credit to small businesses and individuals, fostering entrepreneurship and job creation.

- *Increased Economic Resilience*: Diversifying the banking sector with more community banks can enhance overall economic resilience by reducing dependence on large financial institutions.

- *Challenges in Competition*: Community banks may face challenges competing with larger banks in terms of resources and technology, necessitating supportive policies and frameworks.

7. Enhanced Regulatory Frameworks

Reform: Development of comprehensive and adaptive regulatory frameworks that address the complexities of modern banking and financial innovation.

Impacts:

- *Improved Financial Stability*: Robust regulation can mitigate systemic risks, ensuring the stability of the financial system.

- *Encouragement of Innovation*: Well-designed regulations can promote innovation by providing clear guidelines and reducing uncertainties for new financial technologies.

- *Global Coordination*: Harmonizing regulations across borders can facilitate international cooperation and prevent regulatory arbitrage.

Implementing these reforms requires careful consideration of their potential impacts, both positive and negative. Policymakers must balance the need for financial stability and economic growth with the goals of innovation, inclusion, and sustainability. By doing so, the future of banking and money creation can be shaped to support a more equitable and resilient economy.

The Dark Reality of Banking: Understanding the Creation of Money

The Role of Small Banks and Community Lending in Fostering Economic Stability

Small banks and community lending institutions play a crucial role in fostering economic stability and promoting inclusive growth. Their unique characteristics and localized focus provide several benefits that contribute to the overall health of the financial system and the broader economy.

1. Personalized Banking Services

Focus on Relationships:

Small banks often build strong, personal relationships with their customers. This relationship-based approach allows them to better understand the needs of local businesses and individuals, providing tailored financial solutions that larger banks may overlook.

Enhanced Customer Service:

With a smaller customer base, community banks can offer more personalized and attentive service. This leads to higher customer satisfaction and loyalty, fostering a stable banking environment.

2. Support for Local Economies

Funding Local Enterprises:

Community banks are vital sources of funding for small businesses and local entrepreneurs. By providing credit to these entities, they stimulate local economic activity, create jobs, and support community development.

Retention of Local Wealth:

The profits generated by community banks are often reinvested in the local economy, contributing to the prosperity of the area. This contrasts with large banks, where profits are distributed to distant shareholders.

3. Mitigation of Systemic Risk

Diversification of Financial Services:

Small banks add diversity to the financial sector, reducing the concentration of financial services within a few large institutions. This diversification helps mitigate systemic risk, as problems in one small bank are less likely to trigger widespread financial instability.

Focus on Conservative Lending:

Community banks typically engage in more conservative lending practices. Their focus on relationship lending and thorough understanding of local borrowers reduces the likelihood of risky speculative investments, contributing to financial stability.

4. Promotion of Financial Inclusion

Access to Banking Services:

Community banks play a crucial role in providing banking services to underserved populations, including rural and low-income communities. Their presence ensures that more people have access to essential financial services, promoting financial inclusion and reducing inequality.

Educational Outreach:

Many small banks engage in financial education and outreach programs, helping local residents understand financial management and make informed decisions. This educational role further strengthens the financial stability of communities.

5. Adaptability and Resilience

Responsive to Local Needs:

Community banks can quickly adapt to the changing needs of their local markets. Their agility allows them to respond effectively to local economic conditions, providing support during economic downturns and seizing opportunities for growth.

Strong Community Ties:

The close ties between community banks and their local areas foster a sense of mutual support and resilience. During times of economic stress, these banks are often more willing to work with customers to find solutions, such as loan modifications or extensions.

6. Encouragement of Sustainable Practices

Green Lending Initiatives:

Many community banks are at the forefront of supporting environmentally sustainable projects. By funding local green initiatives and renewable energy projects, they contribute to the transition towards a more sustainable economy.

Local Investment in Sustainability:

Community banks are well-positioned to understand and support local sustainability efforts. Their investments in sustainable practices can drive long-term economic stability and environmental health in their regions.

7. Challenges and Support for Community Banks

Competition with Large Banks:

Community banks often face significant competition from larger banks with more resources. Ensuring a level playing field through supportive regulations and policies is essential to their continued viability.

The Dark Reality of Banking: Understanding the Creation of Money

Technological Advancements:

To remain competitive, community banks must invest in modern technology and digital banking services. Providing support for these technological upgrades can help them better serve their customers and maintain relevance in an increasingly digital world.

Regulatory Support:

Policymakers can support community banks through targeted regulatory measures that recognize their unique role and challenges. Simplified regulatory requirements and access to government programs can enhance their ability to contribute to economic stability.

Small banks and community lending institutions are indispensable to fostering economic stability. Their personalized approach, support for local economies, mitigation of systemic risk, promotion of financial inclusion, adaptability, and commitment to sustainable practices make them critical components of a healthy financial system. By supporting these institutions, policymakers can ensure a more resilient, inclusive, and stable economic future.

TAI-ZAMARAI YASHARAHYALAH

A Poetic Synopsis

"The Gentle Pulse of Small Banks."

In the heart of towns where whispers grow,

Small banks pulse with a steady glow.

Amid the giants, tall and grand,

They hold the dreams of local land.

With hands that know each face and name,

They weave a trust that giants can't claim.

In shops and farms, their seeds are sown,

Investing in fields their own.

No reckless gambles on a distant shore,

They anchor towns, foundations sure.

Through cautious steps, they curb the tide,

Of reckless waves that sweep worldwide.

Their coffers fund the dreams anew,

The Dark Reality of Banking: Understanding the Creation of Money

Of local hands, both old and new.

In every loan, a life takes flight,

They foster hope, they ignite light.

In humble towns, where green fields spread,

They fuel the future, ahead.

In their embrace, communities rise,

Under local banks, beneath clear skies.

Echoes of their care and grace,

In every smiling, familiar face.

These banks, though small, hold grander schemes,

Rooting futures in local dreams.

Recap of Key Points Discussed in Part 1

In our exploration of the dark reality of banking, we've journeyed through the intricate mechanisms that underpin our financial system. Here's a summary of the key insights and revelations from each chapter:

1. The Role of Banks in the Economy:

- Banks are not mere intermediaries but crucial players in the economy, directly influencing money supply.

- The traditional view of banks simply taking deposits and lending them out is misleading. Banks actually create money through lending.

2. Banks as Money Creators:

- Banks create money out of thin air when they issue loans, a process supported by empirical evidence.

- Legal definitions reveal that deposits are essentially loans to banks, emphasizing the transformative power of banks in the monetary system.

3. The Mechanics of Money Creation:

- Detailed how banks record debts and create deposits, effectively generating new money.

The Dark Reality of Banking: Understanding the Creation of Money

- The process of purchasing promissory notes highlights the implications of this money creation mechanism.

4. Economic Impacts of Bank-Created Money:

- When aligned with economic productivity, bank-created money can drive growth without causing inflation.

- However, an excess of money creation can lead to inflation and economic instability, underscoring the need for balance.

5. The Risks of Unproductive Lending:

- Speculative lending by banks can lead to asset bubbles and financial crises.

- Historical case studies illustrate the devastating impacts of such practices on the global economy.

6. Regulatory Challenges and Solutions:

- Current regulations often fail to address the true nature of banks as money creators.

- Historical examples of effective regulation provide lessons for crafting better frameworks.

- Proposals for new regulatory frameworks emphasize the need for stricter oversight and innovative solutions.

7. The Future of Banking and Money Creation:

- Potential reforms include tighter regulations and the promotion of responsible lending practices.

- Small banks and community lending play a vital role in fostering economic stability and supporting local economies.

By understanding the true nature of banking and its profound impact on the economy, we can better navigate the complexities of the financial system. Implementing effective regulations and fostering responsible banking practices are essential steps toward a stable and equitable economic future.

The Dark Reality of Banking: Understanding the Creation of Money

Conclusion to Part 1

The Role of Small Banks and Community Lending in Fostering Stability

Throughout our exploration of the banking system, we've delved into the significant role banks play in money creation and economic dynamics. One critical aspect that emerged is the potential of small banks and community lending to contribute to economic stability.

Empowering Local Economies

Small banks and community lending institutions are uniquely positioned to support local economies. Unlike large commercial banks, which often focus on maximizing profits through speculative investments, small banks tend to prioritize the needs of their communities. They offer personalized services and build long-term relationships with local businesses and individuals. This focus helps ensure that credit is extended to productive ventures, fostering sustainable economic growth.

Mitigating Systemic Risks

The 2008 financial crisis highlighted the dangers of excessive risk-taking by large banks. In contrast, small banks are generally more conservative in their lending practices. By spreading financial resources across numerous small institutions rather than concentrating them in a few large entities, the financial system can become more resilient. Small banks' emphasis on relationship banking and their deeper understanding of local markets can reduce the likelihood of unproductive and speculative lending that leads to asset bubbles and financial instability.

Enhancing Financial Inclusion

Community lending plays a vital role in enhancing financial inclusion. Small banks are often more willing to lend to small and medium-sized enterprises (SMEs), start-ups, and individuals who might be overlooked by larger institutions. This inclusivity not only promotes entrepreneurship and innovation but also helps bridge the gap between different socio-economic groups, contributing to a more equitable distribution of financial resources.

Supporting Economic Diversification

By providing tailored financial products and services, small banks can support economic diversification within their communities. They can identify and finance emerging sectors and local industries that may be neglected by larger banks. This support is crucial for fostering a diverse and

The Dark Reality of Banking: Understanding the Creation of Money

resilient economic base that can withstand broader economic shocks.

Building Trust and Accountability

The close-knit nature of small banks and community lending institutions fosters a higher degree of trust and accountability between lenders and borrowers. This relationship-based approach can lead to more responsible borrowing and lending practices, reducing the risk of defaults and financial crises.

Promoting Sustainable Practices

Small banks often have the flexibility to support sustainable and socially responsible projects that align with community values. By financing green technologies, local agriculture, and socially beneficial enterprises, these banks can contribute to sustainable development goals and the long-term well-being of their communities.

Policy Implications and Recommendations

To maximize the benefits of small banks and community lending, policymakers should consider the following measures:

- Encourage the establishment and growth of small banks through regulatory support and incentives.

- Promote policies that ensure a level playing field for small and large banks, preventing undue competitive disadvantages.

- Foster partnerships between small banks and larger financial institutions to leverage resources and expertise.

- Support financial literacy programs to empower local communities to make informed financial decisions.

Small banks and community lending institutions play a crucial role in fostering economic stability. By prioritizing local needs, enhancing financial inclusion, and supporting sustainable practices, they contribute to a more resilient and equitable financial system. Embracing and strengthening these institutions can help create a stable economic environment that benefits all members of society. Understanding and leveraging the potential of small banks and community lending is a vital step towards achieving a robust and inclusive economy.

A Poetic Deduction

In realms where giants cast their shadows wide,

A quiet force, the small banks, softly strides.

They weave the threads of local dreams and needs,

Nurturing the soil from which our future breeds.

Not bound by whims of speculative might,

The Dark Reality of Banking: Understanding the Creation of Money

They lend with care, each loan a beacon light.

For every seed of trust, they plant and grow,

Ensures a stable, vibrant world we know.

Through whispers of community they speak,

Empowering the strong, supporting the weak.

With every bond of trust, a promise made,

To build a future where no dreams will fade.

In bustling towns where enterprises bloom,

Small banks light paths through any looming gloom.

They know the hearts and minds of those they serve,

With every loan, they steady every nerve.

From crisis' shadows, lessons were unveiled,

That small and steady hands can oft prevail.

Diverse and deep, their roots in local ground,

In every downturn, they remain profound.

So let us honor, in our grand design,

TAI-ZAMARAI YASHARAHYALAH

The quiet force where local hopes entwine.

For in the hands of small banks, dreams take flight,

And guide us to a future clear and bright.

In conclusion, let this truth resound,

In every small bank, a treasure found.

Their humble might and steady, caring ways,

Can forge a path to fairer, brighter days.

"A Symphony of Stability."

In the heart of finance, whispers weave,

Tales of small banks, of what they achieve.

Their role, a symphony in the grand design,

Where community and trust seamlessly entwine.

Not driven by the glittering chase,

But grounded in a steady, measured pace.

They lend not for the fleeting, hollow gain,

But to nurture dreams, through sunshine and rain.

The Dark Reality of Banking: Understanding the Creation of Money

"The Guardians of Balance."

In every ledger, in every quiet note,

The guardians of balance, small banks devote.

To foster growth, not through reckless haste,

But through wisdom, ensuring nothing's waste.

They are the bedrock, the unseen spine,

Supporting structures where our futures shine.

In local hands, they place their faith and care,

Ensuring prosperity is just and fair.

"Threads of Community."

Woven in the fabric of each town,

Are threads of community, of banks renowned.

They stand not as titans, grand and aloof,

But as pillars of trust, steady and proof.

Each loan, a promise to see the future bright,

TAI-ZAMARAI YASHARAHYALAH

Each deposit, a commitment to the light.

For in the embrace of their local kin,

True economic stability begins.

"Steadfastness of Resilience."

Amidst the echoes of crises past,

Small banks stand resilient, steadfast.

They chart a course through turbulent seas,

With principles of prudence, aiming to please.

They are the anchors in uncertain tides,

Guiding with care, where wisdom abides.

In every transaction, in each decision made,

They lay the groundwork for progress to be laid.

"A Vision of Tomorrow."

With a vision cast not just for today,

But for a tomorrow where fairness holds sway.

Small banks and communities, hand in hand,

The Dark Reality of Banking: Understanding the Creation of Money

Creating futures on solid, trusted land.

Through local lending, dreams find their wings,

And stability and prosperity it brings.

For in their humble, consistent way,

They pave the roads to brighter, equitable days.

"The Quiet Revolution."

A quiet revolution, in every deed,

Where small banks tend to every need.

Their impact profound, though subtle it seems,

In every loan, a foundation for dreams.

In unity with community, they stand tall,

Ensuring no dream is too small.

For in their steadfast, local grace,

Lies the essence of a thriving space.

Part 2

PERCEPTION AND REALITY:

An Exploration into the Impacts of Financial Anxiety

The Dark Reality of Banking:
Understanding the Creation of Money

Chapter 8

Perception and Reality

TAI-ZAMARAI YASHARAHYALAH

The Psychological Imapct of Financial Anxiety

Financial anxiety is a pervasive issue that affects individuals across all demographics. It stems from the complex interplay between our perceptions of money, scarcity, and security, and the actual financial realities we face. Understanding how our brains interpret financial situations is crucial for addressing the root causes of financial anxiety and improving overall well-being.

The Brain's Response to Real and Imagined Experiences

The human brain is a powerful organ capable of incredible feats of imagination and perception. Remarkably, it often struggles to distinguish between real and imagined experiences. This phenomenon can have profound implications for how we perceive and react to financial stress.

When we imagine a stressful financial situation, our brains react as if it were real. This triggers the release of stress hormones like cortisol and adrenaline, preparing our bodies for a fight-or-flight response. Over time, chronic activation of this stress response can lead to physical and mental health issues, including anxiety, depression, and cardiovascular problems.

The Dark Reality of Banking: Understanding the Creation of Money

How Fear of Scarcity Triggers Physical and Emotional Stress

Fear of scarcity, whether real or perceived, is a significant driver of financial anxiety. This fear can manifest in various ways, from worrying about not having enough money to cover basic needs to feeling anxious about future financial security. The anticipation of scarcity can be just as debilitating as actual scarcity, leading to a perpetual state of worry and stress.

This constant state of financial fear affects the body's physiological responses. For example, studies have shown that even thinking about financial stress can increase blood pressure, disrupt sleep patterns, and weaken the immune system. The emotional toll of this chronic stress can lead to feelings of helplessness, hopelessness, and a diminished sense of control over one's life.

The Impact of Financial Anxiety on Overall Well-Being

Financial anxiety does not exist in a vacuum; it impacts all aspects of a person's life. It can strain relationships, reduce work productivity, and diminish the quality of life. Individuals with high levels of financial anxiety may avoid dealing with financial issues altogether, leading to a cycle of avoidance and escalating stress.

Moreover, financial anxiety can limit one's ability to enjoy life fully. Constant worry about money can overshadow moments of joy and prevent individuals from pursuing opportunities for personal and professional growth. The pervasive nature of financial anxiety underscores the importance of addressing it holistically.

Breaking the Cycle of Financial Fear

Understanding the psychological impact of financial anxiety is the first step toward breaking the cycle. By recognizing that much of our financial stress is driven by perceptions and not necessarily by reality, we can begin to develop strategies to manage and reduce this anxiety.

1. *Mindfulness and Cognitive Restructuring*: Practicing mindfulness can help individuals stay present and reduce the tendency to catastrophize financial situations. Cognitive restructuring techniques can help reframe negative thoughts about money, replacing them with more realistic and positive ones.

2. *Financial Education and Planning*: Increasing financial literacy and creating a sound financial plan can provide a sense of control and reduce uncertainty. Knowledge empowers individuals to make informed decisions and feel more confident about their financial future.

3. *Seeking Professional Help*: Financial advisors, therapists, and counselors can offer support and guidance in managing financial stress. Professional advice can help individuals

develop coping strategies and create actionable plans to improve their financial situation.

4. *Building a Support Network*: Sharing financial concerns with trusted friends or family members can provide emotional support and practical advice. A strong support network can help alleviate the burden of financial anxiety and offer a sense of community.

By addressing financial anxiety through a combination of psychological and practical approaches, individuals can regain control over their finances and improve their overall well-being. Understanding the powerful connection between perception and reality is key to transforming how we experience and manage financial stress.

The Brain's Response to Real and Imagined Experiences

The human brain is a fascinating and complex organ, equipped with the remarkable ability to process vast amounts of information and create detailed representations of reality. One of its most intriguing capabilities is its difficulty in distinguishing between actual experiences and those vividly imagined. This characteristic has profound implications for how we experience financial anxiety and stress.

The Power of Imagination and Perception

Our brains are wired to react to imagined scenarios almost as intensely as they react to real ones. This is due to the brain's use of similar neural pathways and mechanisms when processing both types of experiences. For example, when we imagine ourselves in a stressful financial situation—like losing a job or facing an unexpected expense—our brains respond as if the scenario were actually happening.

This response involves the activation of the amygdala, the brain's fear center, which triggers the release of stress hormones such as cortisol and adrenaline. These hormones prepare the body for a fight-or-flight response, causing physical reactions like increased heart rate, heightened alertness, and muscle tension.

The Illusion of Scarcity

When people fear financial scarcity, even if the threat is not immediate or realistic, their brains and bodies still react strongly. This imagined fear can lead to chronic stress and anxiety, as the brain continuously perceives a threat to one's financial security. The illusion of scarcity becomes a self-perpetuating cycle, where the anticipation of financial hardship leads to real psychological and physiological stress responses.

The Dark Reality of Banking: Understanding the Creation of Money

For instance, imagining a scenario where one struggles to pay bills can cause as much stress as actually being unable to pay them. The brain's inability to distinguish between the two means that the imagined scenario has real effects on our mental and physical health.

Hormonal Flood and Physical Impact

Every thought and emotion we experience triggers a cascade of hormonal and chemical responses in the body. In the context of financial stress, this means that worrying about money can lead to a continuous release of stress hormones. Over time, this can have several adverse effects:

- *Mental Health:* Chronic stress can contribute to anxiety disorders, depression, and other mental health issues. The constant worry about financial stability can make it difficult to focus, sleep, and enjoy life.

- *Physical Health:* Persistent stress increases the risk of cardiovascular diseases, weakens the immune system, and can cause chronic conditions like hypertension and diabetes.

- *Behavioral Impact:* Financial anxiety can lead to avoidance behaviors, such as procrastinating on financial tasks or avoiding discussions about money, which can exacerbate financial problems.

Real-World Evidence of Perception's Power

Research supports the idea that perception significantly influences our physical and emotional states. For example, studies have shown that visualizing a bright light can cause the pupils to constrict, while imagining darkness can make them dilate. This illustrates how powerful the mind's influence can be over the body's physiological responses.

Similarly, imagining financial stress can lead to real physical reactions, even in the absence of actual financial difficulty. This underscores the importance of managing how we perceive and respond to financial challenges.

Strategies to Manage Financial Perceptions

Understanding the brain's response to real and imagined experiences highlights the need for strategies to manage financial perceptions and reduce stress:

1. *Mindfulness and Visualization*: Practicing mindfulness can help individuals stay grounded in the present moment, reducing the tendency to catastrophize future financial scenarios. Positive visualization techniques can replace negative images with more constructive ones, helping to alleviate stress.

2. *Education and Preparation*: Increasing financial literacy and creating a solid financial plan can help reduce

uncertainty and fear. Knowing that one has a plan in place for potential financial challenges can provide a sense of security and control.

3. *Therapeutic Interventions*: Cognitive-behavioral therapy (CBT) and other therapeutic approaches can help individuals reframe negative thoughts about money and develop healthier coping mechanisms.

4. *Support Systems*: Building a network of supportive friends, family, or financial advisors can provide emotional and practical support, helping to alleviate the burden of financial anxiety.

By acknowledging the brain's powerful role in shaping our financial experiences, we can develop more effective strategies to manage financial anxiety and improve overall well-being. Understanding that perception often creates our reality allows us to approach financial stress with greater awareness and resilience.

TAI-ZAMARAI YASHARAHYALAH

How Fear of Scarcity Triggers Physical and Mental Stress

The fear of scarcity, particularly financial scarcity, is a potent trigger for physical and emotional stress. This fear can dominate an individual's thoughts and behaviors, leading to a cascade of negative consequences that affect overall well-being. Understanding how this fear operates can help individuals and policymakers develop strategies to mitigate its harmful effects.

The Psychological Mechanisms of Scarcity Fear

Fear of scarcity is rooted in the brain's survival mechanisms. When faced with a perceived threat to resources—whether financial, food, or shelter—the brain activates the stress response system. This involves the amygdala, which signals the hypothalamus to initiate the release of stress hormones, primarily cortisol and adrenaline.

These hormones prepare the body to deal with immediate threats by increasing heart rate, blood pressure, and energy supplies. However, when the fear of scarcity becomes chronic, it keeps the body in a prolonged state of heightened alert, leading to various health issues.

The Dark Reality of Banking: Understanding the Creation of Money

Physical Effects of Scarcity Fear

1. *Cardiovascular Problems*: Chronic stress from financial worries can lead to high blood pressure, increased heart rate, and a higher risk of heart attacks and strokes.

2. *Immune System Suppression*: Continuous stress weakens the immune system, making the body more susceptible to infections and illnesses.

3. *Digestive Issues*: Stress can cause or exacerbate gastrointestinal problems, including ulcers, irritable bowel syndrome (IBS), and indigestion.

4. *Sleep Disturbances*: Anxiety about financial security often leads to insomnia or poor-quality sleep, further weakening the body's ability to cope with stress.

Emotional and Behavioral Impact

1. *Anxiety and Depression*: Persistent financial stress is a major contributor to anxiety disorders and depression. The constant worry about making ends meet or future financial stability can overwhelm an individual, leading to feelings of hopelessness and despair.

2. *Cognitive Impairment*: Stress can impair cognitive functions such as memory, attention, and decision-making. This makes it harder to plan, solve problems, and manage finances effectively, creating a vicious cycle of stress and poor financial management.

3. *Behavioral Changes*: The fear of scarcity often leads to maladaptive behaviors. These can include avoidance of financial planning, impulsive spending as a form of temporary relief, or excessive frugality that can reduce quality of life.

4. *Social Isolation:* Financial stress can lead to social withdrawal, as individuals may feel ashamed or embarrassed about their situation. This isolation deprives them of the social support necessary to manage stress effectively.

The Role of Perception in Scarcity Fear

The brain's response to scarcity is not always based on objective reality. Often, the perception of scarcity—whether accurate or not—triggers the same stress responses as actual scarcity. This means that even individuals who are not in immediate financial trouble can experience significant stress if they perceive their financial future as insecure.

For example, media reports about economic downturns or witnessing the financial struggles of peers can exacerbate one's own fears about financial scarcity, even if their personal situation remains stable. This illustrates the power of perception in driving stress responses.

Strategies to Alleviate Scarcity Fear

1. *Financial Education*: Improving financial literacy can help individuals feel more in control of their finances. Understanding budgeting, saving, and investing can reduce uncertainty and build confidence.

The Dark Reality of Banking: Understanding the Creation of Money

2. *Mindfulness Practices*: Techniques such as meditation and mindfulness can help individuals stay present and manage anxiety. These practices can reduce the tendency to catastrophize future financial scenarios.

3. *Therapeutic Support*: Professional therapy, particularly cognitive-behavioral therapy (CBT), can help individuals reframe negative thoughts about money and develop healthier coping mechanisms.

4. *Social Support Networks*: Building strong support networks can provide emotional and practical assistance. Sharing concerns with trusted friends, family, or financial advisors can reduce feelings of isolation and overwhelm.

5. *Positive Visualization*: Instead of focusing on potential negative outcomes, individuals can practice positive visualization to imagine successful financial scenarios. This can help shift the brain's response from fear to proactive problem-solving.

Understanding how the fear of scarcity triggers physical and emotional stress underscores the importance of addressing both the psychological and practical aspects of financial anxiety. By managing perceptions and adopting healthier coping strategies, individuals can mitigate the detrimental effects of financial stress and improve their overall well-being.

TAI-ZAMARAI YASHARAHYALAH

The Impact of Financial Anxiety on Overall Well-Being

Financial anxiety, characterized by constant worry and stress about money, can profoundly affect overall well-being. Its impact extends beyond the bank account, influencing physical health, mental health, relationships, and day-to-day functioning. This section explores the multifaceted ways financial anxiety can degrade quality of life and highlights the importance of addressing this pervasive issue.

Physical Health

1. *Cardiovascular Issues*: Financial anxiety can lead to chronic stress, which is closely linked to cardiovascular problems such as high blood pressure, heart disease, and stroke. The stress hormones released in response to financial worries increase heart rate and blood pressure, putting extra strain on the heart and circulatory system.

2. *Immune System Suppression*: Chronic stress from financial concerns can weaken the immune system, making the body more susceptible to infections and illnesses. This suppression occurs because stress hormones like cortisol can inhibit the immune system's ability to function effectively.

3. *Gastrointestinal Problems*: Stress and anxiety can disrupt normal digestive function, leading to conditions such as irritable bowel syndrome (IBS), ulcers, and acid reflux. Financial stress can exacerbate these conditions, causing significant discomfort and impacting nutrition.

4. *Sleep Disturbances*: Financial anxiety often leads to sleep problems, including insomnia, restless sleep, or frequent waking. Poor sleep quality affects physical health, reducing the body's ability to repair itself and increasing the risk of chronic conditions such as diabetes and obesity.

Mental Health

1. *Anxiety Disorders*: Persistent financial worries are a significant contributor to anxiety disorders. This anxiety can manifest as constant worry, panic attacks, and a feeling of impending doom related to financial security.

2. *Depression*: Financial stress can lead to feelings of hopelessness and helplessness, key features of depression. The ongoing pressure to manage finances, coupled with the fear of economic instability, can result in deep emotional distress and a lack of motivation.

3. *Cognitive Function*: Chronic financial anxiety can impair cognitive functions, including memory, attention, and decision-making abilities. This cognitive load can make it difficult to focus on tasks, leading to decreased productivity and a sense of being overwhelmed.

Relationships

1. *Strain on Personal Relationships*: Financial stress is a common cause of tension in relationships. Disagreements about money can lead to arguments, resentment, and a breakdown in communication. The stress of managing

finances can also reduce the time and energy available for nurturing relationships.

2. *Social Isolation*: Financial anxiety can lead to social withdrawal as individuals may feel ashamed or embarrassed about their financial situation. This isolation deprives them of social support, exacerbating feelings of loneliness and further deteriorating mental health.

3. *Impact on Family Dynamics*: In families, financial stress can create an environment of tension and conflict. Parents preoccupied with financial worries may be less emotionally available to their children, affecting family harmony and children's emotional development.

Daily Functioning

1. *Work Performance:* Financial stress can significantly impact work performance. The cognitive load of worrying about money can reduce focus, creativity, and problem-solving skills. This can lead to decreased productivity and job satisfaction, potentially jeopardizing career advancement.

2. *Lifestyle and Choices*: Financial anxiety often forces individuals to make difficult lifestyle choices, such as cutting back on necessities, foregoing social activities, or delaying important life decisions like buying a home or starting a family. These compromises can reduce overall life satisfaction and well-being.

3. *Behavioral Changes*: Chronic financial anxiety can lead to unhealthy coping mechanisms, such as substance abuse, overeating, or gambling. These behaviors can provide temporary relief but often result in further physical, mental, and financial problems.

The Dark Reality of Banking: Understanding the Creation of Money

Addressing Financial Anxiety

1. *Financial Planning and Education*: Improving financial literacy and engaging in proactive financial planning can help alleviate anxiety. Understanding budgeting, debt management, and investment can provide a sense of control and reduce uncertainty.

2. *Mindfulness and Stress Management*: Techniques such as mindfulness, meditation, and exercise can help manage stress and anxiety. These practices promote relaxation and help individuals stay present, reducing the tendency to ruminate on financial worries.

3. *Therapeutic Interventions*: Professional therapy, including cognitive-behavioral therapy (CBT), can help individuals reframe negative thoughts about money and develop healthier coping strategies. Therapy can also address underlying mental health issues exacerbated by financial stress.

4. *Social Support*: Building and maintaining strong social networks can provide emotional support and practical assistance. Sharing financial concerns with trusted friends, family, or financial advisors can reduce feelings of isolation and provide valuable perspective.

5. *Government and Community Support*: Policies and programs that provide financial assistance, education, and mental health support can play a crucial role in alleviating financial anxiety. Access to resources such as unemployment benefits, affordable healthcare, and financial counseling can help individuals manage financial stress more effectively.

Understanding the broad impact of financial anxiety on overall well-being underscores the importance of addressing this issue comprehensively. By tackling financial anxiety through education, support, and effective stress management techniques, individuals can improve their physical health, mental health, relationships, and overall quality of life.

A Poetic Synopsis

"Perception and Reality: The Psychological Impact of Financial Anxiety."

In the shadows of balance sheets, a silent fear resides,

A whispering ghost of scarcity, where peace and stress collide.

The mind, a potent conjurer, can't tell false from true,

It crafts a world of worry where real and imagined brew.

Each thought a chemical spark, each fear a flood of strain,

Heartbeats race, and pulses quicken, tethered by mental chain.

Financial fears, a heavy cloak, wear down the body's might,

The Dark Reality of Banking: Understanding the Creation of Money

Cardiac strains, and sleepless nights, with no respite in sight.

Immune defenses falter, under chronic stress's load,

Stomach churns and knots with worry, on a winding, weary road.

In the mind, dark clouds gather, anxiety's cruel decree,

Memory fades, and focus shatters, in a storm of misery.

Relationships bear the burden, of this silent, stealthy thief,

Arguments and silent wars, born of financial grief.

Social bonds grow thin and frail, as shameful secrets hide,

Isolation deepens wounds, with no one by your side.

Daily life, a struggle now, as work performance slips,

Creativity is lost to fear, and productivity dips.

Choices narrow, dreams deferred, under pressure's endless grind,

Seeking solace in vices dark, to ease a troubled mind.

But hope can shine through darkest nights, with knowledge as our guide,

TAI-ZAMARAI YASHARAHYALAH

Financial literacy's beacon bright, can turn the anxious tide.

Mindfulness and therapy, can calm the stormy seas,

With social bonds and support strong, find strength amidst the trees.

Policies of compassion, lend a helping hand,

Community and government, together we can stand.

In understanding, we find peace, in unity, we grow,

From the shadows of financial fear, a brighter path can show.

Chapter 9

The Illusion of Scarcity

Understanding the Difference Between Percieved and Actual Scarcity

Scarcity is a concept that pervades economic theories and personal financial anxieties alike. However, the line between perceived scarcity and actual scarcity often blurs, leading to misconceptions and misguided behaviors. To navigate this complex terrain, it is essential to dissect these two forms of scarcity and understand their impacts on our economic and personal lives.

Actual Scarcity:

Actual scarcity refers to the genuine limitation of resources. This is when resources are objectively insufficient to meet the demands. Natural resources like clean water, fossil fuels, and arable land can be examples of actual scarcity, dictated by their physical finiteness and the rate at which they are consumed.

Perceived Scarcity:

Perceived scarcity, on the other hand, is more psychological. It is the belief that resources are limited when, in reality, they may not be. This perception can be influenced by marketing tactics, social comparisons, and economic systems designed to create a sense of urgency and competition.

The Dark Reality of Banking: Understanding the Creation of Money

Economic Impact:

The distinction between actual and perceived scarcity can have profound implications for economic stability and policy-making. For instance, perceived scarcity can drive inflation when consumers rush to purchase goods they believe are in short supply. This was observed during the COVID-19 pandemic when fears of shortages led to stockpiling of items like toilet paper and hand sanitizers, despite sufficient supply chains.

Personal Financial Impact:

On a personal level, perceived scarcity can lead to financial anxiety and poor decision-making. Individuals might hoard money or goods, invest in suboptimal assets, or engage in excessive work hours, fearing future scarcity. This mindset can inhibit financial growth and lead to stress-related health issues.

The Role of Media and Advertising:

Media and advertising play significant roles in shaping perceptions of scarcity. Limited-time offers, exclusive deals, and the portrayal of luxury lifestyles can create a sense of urgency and inadequacy, pushing individuals to spend beyond their means or accumulate debt.

Addressing the Illusion:

To mitigate the effects of perceived scarcity, education and awareness are crucial. Financial literacy programs can help individuals differentiate between actual and perceived scarcity, making informed decisions based on objective assessments rather than fear. Additionally, fostering a culture of abundance and sustainability can shift the focus from competition to cooperation and long-term planning.

By understanding the nuances between perceived and actual scarcity, individuals and policymakers can better navigate economic landscapes, reduce anxiety, and promote a more balanced approach to resource management and financial planning. This understanding lays the groundwork for addressing broader issues of inequality and sustainability, paving the way for a more resilient and equitable society.

The Psychological Mechanisms Behind the FGear of Not Having Enough

The fear of not having enough, often referred to as scarcity mentality, is deeply rooted in psychological mechanisms that influence our thoughts, emotions, and behaviors. Understanding these mechanisms can provide insights into why individuals experience financial anxiety and how this fear can be managed.

The Dark Reality of Banking: Understanding the Creation of Money

1. Evolutionary Roots:

- *Survival Instincts*: Historically, human survival depended on securing sufficient resources such as food, water, and shelter. This evolutionary background ingrains a natural tendency to prioritize resource acquisition and conservation.

- *Fight or Flight Response*: When faced with perceived scarcity, the body's fight-or-flight response is triggered, releasing stress hormones like cortisol and adrenaline. This prepares the body for immediate action but can lead to chronic stress if the perceived threat persists.

2. Cognitive Biases:

- *Loss Aversion*: People tend to fear losses more than they value gains. This bias can make the prospect of financial scarcity feel more threatening than the potential benefits of financial abundance.

- *Availability Heuristic:* The tendency to judge the likelihood of events based on how easily examples come to mind. Media stories about economic downturns or personal anecdotes of financial hardship can amplify the perception of scarcity.

- *Endowment Effect*: People ascribe more value to things merely because they own them. This can lead to an exaggerated fear of losing what one has, even if the actual risk is low.

3. Social and Cultural Influences:

- *Social Comparison*: Constant comparisons with others, fueled by social media and consumer culture, can create a sense of inadequacy and fear of falling behind.

- *Cultural Norms*: Societal norms that equate success with material wealth can exacerbate the fear of not having enough, pushing individuals to strive for more than they need.

4. Emotional Responses:

- *Anxiety and Stress*: The fear of financial scarcity can lead to chronic anxiety and stress, impacting mental and physical health.

- *Shame and Guilt:* Feelings of shame and guilt about one's financial status can deepen the emotional toll of perceived scarcity, leading to a vicious cycle of negative emotions.

5. Behavioral Consequences:

- *Hoarding and Overworking:* In response to scarcity fears, individuals may hoard money or goods, work excessively, or engage in other behaviors aimed at securing resources, often at the expense of their well-being.

- *Risk Aversion:* Fear of financial loss can lead to overly conservative financial decisions, potentially missing out on opportunities for growth and security.

6. Psychological Interventions:

- *Mindfulness and Stress Reduction*: Techniques like mindfulness meditation can help individuals manage stress and reduce anxiety related to scarcity fears.

- *Cognitive Behavioral Therapy (CBT)*: CBT can help individuals reframe their thoughts and challenge irrational beliefs about scarcity, fostering a more balanced perspective.

- *Financial Education*: Increasing financial literacy can empower individuals to make informed decisions, reducing the fear of the unknown and promoting a sense of control over one's financial future.

By recognizing and addressing these psychological mechanisms, individuals can develop healthier attitudes towards money and resources, reducing the fear of not having enough and fostering a sense of financial well-being.

How Societal Narratives Around Scarcity Influence Individual Behaviour

Societal narratives around scarcity—shaped by cultural norms, media representations, economic policies, and social expectations—play a significant role in influencing individual behavior. These narratives can perpetuate fear, anxiety, and a sense of perpetual inadequacy, affecting how people perceive and manage their resources. Understanding these influences is crucial for recognizing the broader impact of societal messaging on personal well-being and financial decisions.

1. Cultural Norms and Values:

- *Materialism and Consumerism*: Societal emphasis on material success and consumerism reinforces the idea that more possessions equate to higher status and happiness. This drives individuals to constantly seek more, fearing that they will fall behind if they don't keep up with societal standards.

- *Success Metrics:* Success is often measured by financial wealth and material possessions, rather than personal fulfillment or community contributions. This creates pressure to accumulate wealth and assets, reinforcing the scarcity mindset.

2. Media Representations:

- *Fear-Based Reporting*: Media often highlights economic downturns, job losses, and financial crises, which can amplify fears of scarcity. Sensationalist headlines and stories about financial disasters create a heightened sense of insecurity.

- *Advertising and Marketing*: Advertisements frequently exploit scarcity principles, such as limited-time offers or exclusive deals, to drive consumer behavior. This tactic reinforces the belief that resources are limited and must be acquired quickly to avoid missing out.

The Dark Reality of Banking: Understanding the Creation of Money

3. Economic Policies and Practices:

- *Inequality and Access*: Economic policies that create or sustain inequality can contribute to the perception of scarcity. When a small percentage of the population holds a significant portion of the wealth, the majority may feel that resources are scarce and unattainable.

- *Job Insecurity:* Shifts in the job market, such as the rise of gig economy jobs and the decline of stable, long-term employment, can make individuals feel that financial stability is elusive, reinforcing the scarcity narrative.

4. Social Expectations and Peer Pressure:

- *Keeping Up with Peers:* Social media platforms showcase idealized versions of life, where peers appear to be constantly achieving and acquiring more. This can lead to unhealthy comparisons and the pressure to keep up, fostering a sense of scarcity.

- *Social Status and Competition*: In competitive environments, individuals may feel that they must continuously strive for more resources to maintain or improve their social status. This competition can lead to stress and anxiety about not having enough.

5. Psychological Effects:

- *Internalized Scarcity:* Constant exposure to scarcity narratives can lead individuals to internalize these messages, affecting their self-worth and decision-making processes.

They may develop a chronic sense of inadequacy and fear of loss.

- *Behavioral Responses:* The perception of scarcity can drive behaviors such as hoarding, overworking, and risk aversion. These behaviors are attempts to mitigate the fear of not having enough but often result in increased stress and reduced well-being.

6. Community and Support Systems:

- *Erosion of Community Bonds:* Narratives that emphasize individual success over community well-being can erode social support systems, leaving individuals feeling isolated and more susceptible to scarcity fears.

- *Collective Solutions*: Conversely, communities that emphasize collective well-being and mutual support can help counteract scarcity narratives. Sharing resources and supporting each other can foster a sense of abundance and security.

7. Education and Awareness:

- *Financial Literacy:* Promoting financial literacy can empower individuals to make informed decisions and feel more in control of their resources. Understanding how to manage money effectively can reduce the fear of scarcity.

- *Mindset Shifts:* Encouraging mindset shifts from scarcity to abundance can help individuals reframe their perceptions. Practices such as gratitude journaling and focusing on what one has, rather than what one lacks, can cultivate a sense of sufficiency.

The Dark Reality of Banking: Understanding the Creation of Money

By recognizing the powerful influence of societal narratives around scarcity, individuals can begin to challenge and change these perceptions. Shifting the focus from fear and competition to abundance and collaboration can foster healthier behaviors and improve overall well-being.

A Poetic Synopsis

"Scarcity's Illusion."

In a world spun by tales of lack,

Where fear of loss paints the track,

Society's whispers shape our mind,

To see abundance, yet feel confined.

Cultural norms that bid us chase,

Endless goods, a ceaseless race,

Media stirs the pot of fear,

Limited offers, time draws near.

Economic rules that split the wealth,

TAI-ZAMARAI YASHARAHYALAH

Leave many feeling poor in stealth,

Social status, peer's bright light,

Push us deeper into the night.

Job security fades to mist,

In a gig economy's twist,

In this dance of fleeting chance,

Scarcity's shadow seems to enhance.

But deeper truths lie in our hearts,

Communal ties where sharing starts,

Education breaks the spell,

Of scarcity's relentless knell.

Shift the gaze from what we miss,

To gratitude, a state of bliss,

For in the bonds of human kind,

True abundance we can find.

Scarcity's a crafted veil,

Lift it, and let true wealth prevail,
□

The Dark Reality of Banking: Understanding the Creation of Money

For when we share and give, we see,

The richness of community.

Chapter 10

The Science of Perception

How Thoughts and Perception Create Our Reality

Our thoughts and perceptions play a critical role in shaping our reality. This concept is rooted in the understanding that our brain processes both actual and imagined experiences similarly. Here's a closer look at how this fascinating process works:

1. Neuroscience of Perception:

- The brain does not distinguish between a real event and a vividly imagined one. When you think of a sunny day, your brain activates in much the same way as it does when you are actually in the sun. Similarly, imagining a dark room can cause your pupils to contract, just as they would in actual darkness.

2. Cognitive Biases:

- Our perceptions are influenced by cognitive biases—mental shortcuts that help us make sense of the world. These biases can skew our understanding of reality, often causing us to overestimate threats or shortages, leading to unnecessary stress and anxiety.

3. Perception and Emotion:

- Emotions are powerful drivers of perception. When we are anxious or fearful, our brain is more likely to focus on negative aspects of our environment, reinforcing a sense of scarcity or danger.

4. The Feedback Loop:

- Thoughts create emotions, which in turn reinforce thoughts in a continuous feedback loop. For example, worrying about financial insecurity can lead to feelings of stress and anxiety, which then make us more likely to perceive our situation as dire, regardless of the actual circumstances.

5. Hormonal Responses:

- Every thought we have triggers a corresponding release of hormones and neurotransmitters. Positive thoughts can lead to the release of dopamine and serotonin, promoting feelings of well-being, while negative thoughts can flood the body with cortisol and adrenaline, heightening stress and anxiety.

Understanding the science of perception helps us recognize that much of our experience of scarcity or abundance is constructed in the mind. By changing our thought patterns and perceptions, we can alter our reality, moving from a state of constant fear and anxiety to one of peace and contentment.

The Biological Responses to Imagined Versus Real Experiences

Our brain's remarkable ability to blur the lines between real and imagined experiences is at the heart of our perception. This ability has profound implications for our mental and physical well-being. Here's how the brain and body respond to these experiences:

1. Neurochemical Reactions:

- When we think about a pleasurable experience, our brain releases dopamine, the "feel-good" neurotransmitter. Conversely, imagining a stressful scenario triggers the release of cortisol and adrenaline, just as it would in a real-life stressful situation. These neurochemicals prepare the body for action, whether the threat is real or imagined.

2. Physiological Responses:

- Imagined experiences can elicit physical reactions similar to those caused by real experiences. For instance, thinking about a bright light can cause pupil dilation, while imagining darkness causes pupil contraction. This demonstrates the direct influence of thoughts on our body's autonomic responses.

3. The Limbic System:

- The limbic system, which includes the amygdala and hippocampus, plays a key role in emotional processing. It responds to both real and imagined threats by activating the fight-or-flight response. This can lead to increased heart rate, rapid breathing, and heightened alertness, regardless of whether the danger is real.

4. Hormonal Flood:

- The hypothalamus-pituitary-adrenal (HPA) axis is activated by stress, whether actual or perceived. This leads to the release of cortisol, which prepares the body to deal with potential threats. Chronic activation of this system, due to ongoing imagined threats, can lead to long-term health issues such as hypertension and weakened immune function.

5. Muscle Tension:

- Thinking about stressful situations can cause muscle tension, as the body prepares to respond to a perceived threat. This can result in chronic pain and tension headaches if the imagined threats are frequent and persistent.

6. Energy Consumption:

- The brain uses a significant amount of energy to process imagined experiences. This can lead to mental fatigue, impacting cognitive functions such as memory, concentration, and decision-making.

7. Mind-Body Connection:

- The placebo effect is a powerful demonstration of how imagined experiences can lead to real biological changes. Believing that a treatment will work can trigger the body's healing mechanisms, even if the treatment is inactive. This underscores the power of belief and perception in shaping our physical health.

Understanding the biological responses to imagined versus real experiences highlights the importance of managing our thoughts and perceptions. By cultivating a more positive and realistic mindset, we can mitigate unnecessary stress and improve our overall health and well-being.

Examples of Perception Affecting Physiological Responses

The power of perception to influence physiological responses is a fascinating aspect of human biology. Here are some compelling examples:

1. Pupil Dilation and Contraction:

- *Bright Light and Darkness*: When a person imagines themselves in a bright light, their pupils may dilate as if they are actually in a well-lit environment. Conversely, imagining being in complete darkness can cause the pupils to contract, demonstrating how mental imagery can affect the autonomic nervous system.

2. Heart Rate Variability:

- *Stressful Thoughts:* Thinking about a stressful situation, such as an upcoming exam or a difficult conversation, can increase heart rate and blood pressure. This mirrors the body's response to real-life stressors, preparing the body for fight-or-flight even when no physical threat is present.

- *Relaxation Techniques*: On the other hand, practicing relaxation techniques such as guided imagery or meditation can lead to a decrease in heart rate and blood pressure, promoting a state of calm and relaxation.

3. Muscle Tension:

- *Imagining Physical Activity:* Visualizing engaging in physical activities, like lifting weights or running, can cause slight muscle contractions and increased muscle tone. Athletes often use this technique to prepare their bodies for performance.

- *Stress-Induced Tension:* Simply imagining a stressful event can lead to increased muscle tension, particularly in the neck and shoulders, which can result in tension headaches or chronic pain over time.

4. Sweat Response:

- *Fear and Anxiety:* Imagining a fearful scenario, such as standing at the edge of a cliff or giving a public speech, can activate the sympathetic nervous system, leading to sweating and other signs of anxiety. This is often used in psychological studies to measure stress responses.

- *Relaxing Imagery:* Visualizing a serene and calming scene, like a peaceful beach, can reduce sweating and promote a sense of tranquility.

5. Gastrointestinal Responses:

- *Anticipation of Food:* Thinking about food, especially favorite dishes, can stimulate salivation and digestive enzyme production as the body prepares for eating. This is a demonstration of the cephalic phase of digestion, where the sight, smell, or thought of food triggers digestive processes.

- *Stress and Digestion:* Conversely, imagining stressful situations can inhibit digestive processes, leading to symptoms like nausea or stomach cramps, as the body diverts energy away from digestion to prepare for perceived threats.

6. Immune System Response:

- *Placebo Effect*: Believing in the efficacy of a treatment can lead to real physiological improvements, such as reduced pain or faster recovery from illness. This placebo effect demonstrates the profound impact of positive perception on the body's healing processes.

- *Nocebo Effect:* Similarly, negative expectations can lead to worsening symptoms, illustrating how detrimental thoughts can adversely affect health.

7. Hormonal Fluctuations:

- *Stress Hormones:* Imagining a high-stress situation can increase cortisol and adrenaline levels, preparing the body for a fight-or-flight response. Chronic stress thoughts can keep these hormone levels elevated, leading to long-term health issues such as anxiety, depression, and metabolic disorders.

- *Positive Visualization*: Conversely, positive visualization and affirmations can reduce stress hormone levels and promote the release of endorphins and oxytocin, fostering a sense of well-being and happiness.

These examples illustrate the profound influence of perception on our physiological state. Understanding and harnessing this mind-body connection can be a powerful tool in managing stress, enhancing well-being, and improving overall health.

A Poetic Synopsis

"Perception's Power:"

In the theater of the mind, where shadows dance and play,

The Dark Reality of Banking: Understanding the Creation of Money

Perception weaves its potent spell, in night and light of day.

The brain, a master alchemist, blends thought with deep belief,

Transmuting fear to felt distress, or joy to sweet relief.

Imagined suns can warm the heart, dilate the seeking eyes,

While phantoms of the darkest night bring narrowing surprise.

A stress thought churns the inner seas, makes hearts beat wild and fast,

Yet tranquil scenes of calm repose bring peace that's made to last.

Muscles tense with phantom weights, or ease with thoughts of peace,

Sweat pours from fear's imagined heights, then dries as tensions cease.

The food we crave in silent dreams sparks salivation's start,

While stress can twist and knot the gut, wrenching from the heart.

The mind's belief, in potent pills, can heal or bring despair,

Placebo's grace, nocebo's curse, show thoughts laid raw and bare.

TAI-ZAMARAI YASHARAHYALAH

Stress hormones surge from mere concern, like predators at night,

Yet joyful thoughts can flood with bliss, bringing pure delight.

So know this well, that thoughts alone can craft the world we see,

Perception's power shapes our lives, molds our reality.

Harness this force, let wisdom guide, to build a life of peace,

For every thought that's wisely chosen brings endless sweet release.

The Dark Reality of Banking:
Understanding the Creation of Money

Chapter 11

Emotional and Physical Health in Financial Matters

The Link Between Financial Stress and Physical Health

Financial stress is not just a matter of the mind; it leaves tangible marks on the body, influencing physical health in profound ways. Here are key points to understand this link:

1. Stress Hormones and Physical Health

- Financial anxiety triggers the release of stress hormones like cortisol and adrenaline.

- Chronic elevation of these hormones can lead to a host of health issues, including hypertension, heart disease, and diabetes.

2. Immune System Suppression

- Prolonged financial stress weakens the immune system, making the body more susceptible to infections and illnesses.

- High stress levels can exacerbate autoimmune conditions, leading to more frequent flare-ups.

3. Sleep Disturbances

The Dark Reality of Banking: Understanding the Creation of Money

- Worrying about money often leads to insomnia or poor-quality sleep, which impairs cognitive function and emotional regulation.

- Lack of sleep can further degrade physical health, contributing to conditions like obesity and cardiovascular diseases.

4. Mental Health Consequences

- Financial stress is a significant risk factor for mental health disorders such as anxiety, depression, and even substance abuse.

- The mental strain can reduce the ability to manage stress, creating a vicious cycle of deteriorating mental and physical health.

5. Behavioral Health Risks

- Financial pressure can lead to unhealthy coping mechanisms such as overeating, smoking, or excessive alcohol consumption.

- These behaviors increase the risk of developing chronic diseases and further exacerbate physical health problems.

6. Health Care Access and Quality

- Financial instability often limits access to healthcare services and preventive care, leading to delayed diagnoses and untreated conditions.

- Individuals under financial stress may also skip medications or necessary treatments to save money, worsening their health outcomes.

7. Relationships and Social Health

- Financial stress can strain relationships, leading to social isolation and reduced emotional support.

- Poor social health and strained relationships can contribute to a sense of loneliness and exacerbate both mental and physical health issues.

Understanding the deep connection between financial health and overall well-being is crucial. By recognizing and addressing financial stress, individuals can take proactive steps to protect both their mental and physical health, leading to a more balanced and healthier life.

The Dark Reality of Banking: Understanding the Creation of Money

How Chronic Stress from Financial Worries Impacts Bodily Functions

Chronic stress from financial worries has a profound and pervasive impact on bodily functions, affecting nearly every system in the body. Here's how this stress manifests physically:

1. Cardiovascular System

- *Increased Heart Rate and Blood Pressure*: Chronic financial stress causes persistent activation of the sympathetic nervous system, leading to elevated heart rate and blood pressure. Over time, this can result in hypertension and increase the risk of heart attacks and strokes.

- *Atherosclerosis*: Prolonged stress contributes to the buildup of plaque in arteries, known as atherosclerosis, which can restrict blood flow and lead to serious cardiovascular diseases.

2. Digestive System

- *Gastrointestinal Issues:* Stress affects the digestive system, leading to symptoms such as stomach aches, indigestion, diarrhea, or constipation. Chronic stress can exacerbate conditions like irritable bowel syndrome (IBS) and peptic ulcers.

- *Appetite Changes*: Financial stress can cause significant changes in appetite, leading to overeating or loss of appetite, both of which can affect nutrition and overall health.

3. Immune System

- *Suppressed Immune Response*: The body's immune response is weakened under chronic stress, making individuals more susceptible to infections and illnesses. This suppression also means that wounds may heal more slowly.

- *Inflammation*: Stress can lead to increased inflammation in the body, contributing to a range of chronic illnesses such as arthritis, diabetes, and cardiovascular diseases.

4. Musculoskeletal System

- *Muscle Tension and Pain*: Financial worries can cause muscle tension, particularly in the neck, shoulders, and back. This can lead to chronic pain conditions, headaches, and migraines.

- *Risk of Injury*: Chronic stress can impair coordination and increase the risk of injuries, as tense muscles are more prone to strains and sprains.

5. Respiratory System

- *Breathing Difficulties:* Stress can cause shortness of breath or hyperventilation, which may exacerbate respiratory conditions like asthma and chronic obstructive pulmonary disease (COPD).

- *Panic Attacks*: Severe anxiety can trigger panic attacks, characterized by intense fear, rapid breathing, and heart palpitations.

6. Endocrine System

- *Hormonal Imbalance:* Chronic stress disrupts the balance of hormones, including cortisol and adrenaline. Elevated cortisol levels can lead to weight gain, particularly around the abdomen, and contribute to conditions like diabetes and metabolic syndrome.

- *Thyroid Dysfunction*: Prolonged stress can impact thyroid function, potentially leading to hypothyroidism or hyperthyroidism, both of which affect metabolism and energy levels.

7. Nervous System

- *Autonomic Nervous System Overload*: Chronic financial stress keeps the body in a constant state of 'fight or flight,' taxing the autonomic nervous system. This persistent state of alertness can lead to fatigue, difficulty concentrating, and memory problems.

- *Neurotransmitter Imbalance:* Stress affects the levels of neurotransmitters such as serotonin and dopamine, which play key roles in mood regulation and overall mental health.

8. Reproductive System

- *Menstrual Irregularities:* In women, chronic stress can lead to irregular menstrual cycles, more painful periods, and exacerbated premenstrual syndrome (PMS) symptoms.

- *Reduced Libido and Fertility:* Financial worries can reduce libido and impact fertility in both men and women. In men, stress can affect sperm production and erectile function.

9. Skin and Hair

- *Skin Problems:* Stress can trigger or worsen skin conditions such as eczema, psoriasis, and acne. It can also lead to hives and other stress-induced skin reactions.

- *Hair Loss:* Chronic stress is a significant factor in hair loss conditions like telogen effluvium, where hair follicles enter a resting phase and hair sheds excessively.

Understanding the wide-reaching impacts of financial stress on bodily functions highlights the importance of managing stress and seeking help to address financial concerns. Taking steps to reduce financial anxiety can significantly improve physical health and overall quality of life.

The Dark Reality of Banking:
Understanding the Creation of Money

Strategies for Managing Anxiety to Improve Health Outcomes

anaging financial anxiety is crucial for improving both mental and physical health. Here are effective strategies to help reduce financial stress and its associated health impacts:

1. Financial Planning and Budgeting

- *Create a Budget*: Develop a detailed budget to track income, expenses, and savings. A clear understanding of your financial situation can reduce anxiety.

- *Emergency Fund:* Build an emergency fund to cover unexpected expenses, providing a financial safety net and peace of mind.

- *Debt Management:* Develop a plan to pay off debts systematically, prioritizing high-interest debts first.

2. Professional Financial Advice

- *Financial Advisor:* Consult with a financial advisor to create a long-term financial plan tailored to your goals and situation.

- *Credit Counseling:* Seek help from a credit counselor if struggling with debt. They can provide strategies for managing and reducing debt.

3. Education and Information

- *Financial Literacy*: Improve your financial literacy through books, online courses, and workshops. Understanding financial concepts can empower you to make better decisions.

- *Stay Informed:* Keep up with economic trends and changes in financial regulations to better manage your finances.

4. Stress Management Techniques

- *Mindfulness and Meditation*: Practice mindfulness and meditation to reduce anxiety and promote relaxation. These techniques can help you stay present and manage stress more effectively.

- *Physical Activity*: Engage in regular physical exercise, which can reduce stress hormones and improve mood.

- *Breathing Exercises:* Use deep breathing exercises to calm your nervous system and reduce acute stress.

5. Healthy Lifestyle Choices

- *Balanced Diet:* Maintain a healthy diet to support overall well-being and reduce the physical impacts of stress.

- *Adequate Sleep:* Ensure you get enough sleep each night, as rest is crucial for managing stress and maintaining health.

- *Cut Out/ Limit Caffeine and Alcohol*: Avoid/reduce intake of caffeine and alcohol, which can exacerbate anxiety and disrupt sleep.

6. Emotional and Social Support

- *Therapy and Counseling*: Consider therapy or counseling to address financial anxiety and its emotional impacts. Cognitive-behavioral therapy (CBT) can be particularly effective.

- *Support Network*: Lean on trusted friends, family, or support groups for emotional support and practical advice.

7. Positive Financial Habits

- *Set Realistic Goals*: Set achievable financial goals to stay motivated and track your progress.

- *Celebrate Milestones*: Acknowledge and celebrate financial milestones, no matter how small, to stay positive and motivated.

- *Avoid Comparisons*: Focus on your financial journey rather than comparing yourself to others, which can increase anxiety.

8. Mindset and Perspective

- *Gratitude Practice*: "Your attitude determines your altitude." Cultivate gratitude by focusing on what you have rather than what you lack. This can shift your mindset from scarcity to abundance.

- *Focus on Control*: Concentrate on aspects of your finances that you can control, rather than worrying about uncertainties.

- *Long-Term Perspective*: Adopt a long-term perspective on finances, understanding that building wealth and financial stability takes time.

9. Digital Tools and Resources

- *Budgeting Apps:* Use budgeting and financial planning apps to track expenses, manage debts, and save money efficiently.

- *Online Resources:* Utilize online resources and communities for financial advice, tips, and support.

Implementing these strategies can help manage financial anxiety, improve mental and physical health, and lead to a more stable and fulfilling financial future. By taking proactive steps to address financial stress, individuals can significantly enhance their overall well-being.

A Poetic Synopsis

"Emotional and Physical Health in Financial Matters."

In the labyrinth of ledger lines, where numbers tell a tale,

The heart beats anxious rhythms, where calm should prevail.

☐

The Dark Reality of Banking: Understanding the Creation of Money

The weight of coins and currency, heavy on the soul,

Disturbs the mind's tranquility, extracts a costly toll.

Yet in this storm of figures, there lies a beacon bright,

A path through prudent planning, a way to turn the night.

With budgets carved from patience, and wisdom as our guide,

We build a sturdy vessel to ride the financial tide.

Consult the sages of finance, let their counsel steer your way,

From debts and shadowed worries, towards a clearer day.

Embrace the light of learning, let knowledge be your shield,

For in the grasp of understanding, the strongest fears must yield.

Through mindful breaths and movement, through calm and steady beat,

We find the strength to conquer, the anxious mind's deceit.

The body's health, a temple, through which our peace must flow,

With every balanced measure, our inner gardens grow.

TAI-ZAMARAI YASHARAHYALAH

Seek solace in the circle, of friends and family dear,

In shared support and laughter, the shadows disappear.

Celebrate the milestones, the small triumphs on the path,

For each step forward taken, dispels the stormy wrath.

In gratitude's warm embrace, our hearts begin to see,

That wealth is more than riches, it's in our being free.

Free from the binds of worry, free from the fears we face,

To live a life in balance, in harmony, in grace.

So let us chart the waters, with hope and courage strong,

For in the quest for balance, our spirits shall belong.

To a realm where health and wisdom, in unity are found,

A haven built on prudent care, where peace and strength abound.

The Dark Reality of Banking:
Understanding the Creation of Money

Chapter 12

Breaking Free from the Cycle of Financial Fear

Techniques for Shifting Perception and Reducing Financial Stress

Financial fear can feel like an unending cycle, but with deliberate strategies, it is possible to shift perceptions and significantly reduce stress. This chapter explores various techniques and approaches to help individuals break free from financial anxiety and cultivate a healthier relationship with money.

Mindfulness and Meditation

1. *Mindfulness Practices:*

- *Awareness of Thoughts*: Recognize and observe thoughts about money without judgment.

- *Present Moment Focus*: Concentrate on the present rather than worrying about future financial issues.

2. Meditation Techniques:

- *Guided Meditations:* Use guided audio to focus on financial abundance and stability.

- *Breathing Exercises:* Implement deep breathing to calm the mind and reduce stress.

Cognitive Behavioral Techniques

1. Identifying Negative Thoughts:

- *Cognitive Restructuring:* Challenge and reframe negative thoughts about money.

- *Positive Affirmations:* Replace negative self-talk with positive affirmations regarding financial capability.

2. Behavioral Interventions:

- *Setting Realistic Goals:* Establish achievable financial goals to build confidence.

- *Small Wins*: Celebrate small financial achievements to build momentum.

Financial Literacy and Education

1. Understanding Finances:

- *Budgeting Skills:* Learn and implement effective budgeting techniques.

- *Debt Management:* Gain knowledge about managing and reducing debt.

2. Educational Resources:

- *Workshops and Seminars*: Attend financial literacy workshops and seminars.

- *Online Courses:* Utilize online courses to enhance financial understanding.

Professional Support

1. Financial Advisors:

- **Consultation**: Seek advice from certified financial planners to create a tailored financial plan.

- **Investment Guidance**: Get help with investment strategies to build wealth.

2. Therapeutic Support:

- *Financial Therapists:* Engage with therapists specializing in financial stress.

- *Support Groups*: Join support groups for shared experiences and strategies.

The Dark Reality of Banking: Understanding the Creation of Money

Lifestyle Changes

1. Healthy Living:

- *Exercise and Nutrition*: Maintain a healthy lifestyle to boost overall well-being and reduce stress.

- *Sleep Hygiene*: Ensure adequate and quality sleep to manage stress better.

2. Work-Life Balance:

- *Boundary Setting:* Set boundaries to avoid burnout and maintain balance.

- *Leisure Activities*: Engage in hobbies and activities that bring joy and relaxation.

Building a Support Network

1. Family and Friends:

- *Open Communication*: Talk openly about financial concerns with trusted individuals.

- *Mutual Support*: Create a support system with family and friends to share resources and advice.

2. Community Resources:

- *Non-Profit Organizations*: Utilize community resources for financial counseling and support.

- *Local Workshops*: Participate in local workshops and groups focused on financial health.

By integrating these techniques and approaches, individuals can shift their perception of money and reduce the stress associated with financial fears. Breaking free from the cycle of financial anxiety requires a holistic approach, combining mindfulness, education, professional support, and a strong support network.

Mindfulness and Cognitive-Behavioural Strategies to Alter Thought Patterns

Mindfulness Practices

1. Awareness of Thoughts:

- *Observation*: Take time each day to sit quietly and observe your thoughts about money. Notice any patterns or recurring themes without trying to change them. Simply being aware of these thoughts can begin to reduce their power over you.

- *Non-Judgmental Attitude*: Approach your thoughts with curiosity rather than criticism. Understand that having negative thoughts about money is normal, and the goal is to observe them without getting emotionally entangled.

2. Present Moment Focus:

- *Breathing Exercises:* Focus on your breath to anchor yourself in the present moment. Simple exercises like counting your breaths or deep abdominal breathing can help calm the mind and reduce anxiety.

- *Grounding Techniques:* Engage in activities that bring you into the present, such as mindful walking, paying attention to the sights and sounds around you, or doing a body scan meditation to connect with physical sensations.

Cognitive-Behavioral Techniques

1. Identifying Negative Thoughts:

- *Thought Records*: Keep a journal where you write down negative thoughts related to money as they occur. Identify the situations that trigger these thoughts and the emotions that accompany them.

- *Challenge Your Thoughts*: Once you have identified negative thoughts, challenge their validity. Ask yourself questions like, "Is this thought based on facts or assumptions?" and "What evidence do I have to support or refute this thought?"

2. Reframing and Positive Affirmations:

- *Cognitive Restructuring*: Replace negative thoughts with more realistic and positive ones. For instance, if you think, "I'll never get out of debt," reframe it to, "I am taking steps every day to reduce my debt and improve my financial situation."

- *Positive Affirmations:* Create and regularly recite affirmations that reinforce a positive mindset about money. Examples include, "I am capable of managing my finances effectively," and "I attract abundance and financial security."

3. Behavioral Interventions:

- *Setting Realistic Goals*: Break down larger financial goals into smaller, manageable tasks. Achieving these smaller goals can build confidence and provide a sense of accomplishment.

- *Action Plans*: Develop specific action plans for your financial goals. This might include creating a budget, setting up a savings plan, or seeking professional financial advice. Having a clear plan can reduce anxiety and create a sense of control.

4. Exposure Therapy:

- *Facing Financial Fears*: Gradually expose yourself to financial situations that cause anxiety. For example, if checking your bank account balance is stressful, set aside a specific time each week to do it, gradually increasing the frequency as your comfort level improves.

- *Desensitization*: Pair exposure with relaxation techniques to reduce the emotional impact of financial stressors. Over time, this can help diminish the anxiety associated with these situations.

The Dark Reality of Banking: Understanding the Creation of Money

Combining Mindfulness and CBT

1. Mindful Cognitive Reframing:

- *Present-Focused Reframing*: Use mindfulness to stay grounded while challenging and reframing negative thoughts. For instance, practice deep breathing while working through cognitive restructuring exercises.

- Integration Practices: Incorporate mindfulness into your daily CBT exercises. Start your thought records with a few minutes of mindfulness meditation to enhance clarity and focus.

2. Mindfulness-Based Stress Reduction (MBSR):

- *Structured Programs*: Participate in MBSR programs that combine mindfulness meditation with cognitive-behavioral strategies. These programs can provide structured support and guidance in reducing financial stress.

- *Daily Practice*: Commit to a daily mindfulness and CBT practice. Even a few minutes each day can lead to significant improvements in managing financial anxiety and altering thought patterns.

By integrating mindfulness and cognitive-behavioral strategies, individuals can develop a more balanced and less stressful relationship with money. These techniques help in recognizing and altering negative thought patterns, reducing anxiety, and fostering a mindset of financial well-being.

Success Stories of Individuals Overcoming Financial Anxiety

Mimi's Journey to Financial Peace

Mimi, an entrepreneur, artist, singer songwriter, freelance graphic designer, author and owner of Luxury Actually© clothing brand, had always been anxious about her finances. Despite having so many skill sets, she constantly worried about unexpected expenses and her unpaid overdraft which accumulated interests every month. Her anxiety led to her taking initiative to change her situation, Mimi sought help from a trusted financial advisor who introduced her to mindfulness and cognitive-behavioral strategies.

Mindfulness Practices: Mimi started practicing daily mindfulness meditation, focusing on her breath and grounding herself in the present moment--She called this H.E.R (Healing Every Rise). This helped her become more aware of her financial fears without letting them control her.

Cognitive-Behavioral Techniques: She began keeping a thought journal, identifying and challenging her negative thoughts about money. For instance, she replaced "My finances are a mess, how will I ever get out of debt?" with "I am making steady progress towards paying off my overdraft." She recognised the power of her thoughts, words and intentions, directing them to produce the reality she desires.

The Dark Reality of Banking: Understanding the Creation of Money

Behavioral Interventions: Mimi set realistic financial goals, such as creating a budget and setting aside a small amount for savings each month. She gradually faced her fear of checking her bank balance by setting a weekly routine to review her finances.

Outcome: Over time, Mimi's anxiety diminished. She felt more in control of her financial situation and experienced significant improvements in her sleep and overall health. Her journey inspired her to help others by sharing her story and advocating for financial literacy education in her community.

Zamar's Path to Financial Freedom

Zamar, a freelance Entrepreneur and self published author, struggled with irregular income and the constant stress of making ends meet. The unpredictability of his earnings made it difficult for him to plan for the future, leading to financial anxiety. Zamar uses cognitive-behavioral techniques and mindfulness practices to affirm his greatness and his unwavering abilities to navigate any storm that comes his way.

Mindfulness Practices: Zamar adopted a daily mindfulness practice, which included meditation and daily mindful exercise sessions he called H.I.M. (Healing in Motion). This helped him stay present and focused, ready to face any challenges on a daily basis, eliminate any worries about future financial uncertainties.

Cognitive-Behavioral Techniques: He started using thought records to identify and reframe his negative beliefs about money. Instead of thinking, "I'll never have a stable income," he began to affirm, "I am capable of managing my finances and create my desired reality, even with a fluctuating income."

"I will use what I have to create the life I want, and nothing can stop me. Whatever or whomever tries to stop my destiny, will be instrumental in causing it to be. I am."

Behavioral Interventions: Zamar implemented a budgeting system tailored to his variable income. He set aside funds during high-earning months to cover expenses during lean periods. He also sought out additional freelance opportunities to diversify his income streams.

Outcome: Zamar's proactive approach to managing his finances significantly reduced his anxiety. He felt empowered and more confident in his ability to handle financial challenges. His success story encouraged other freelancers in his network to adopt similar strategies, fostering a supportive community.

These success stories highlight the transformative power of mindfulness and cognitive-behavioral techniques in overcoming financial anxiety. By adopting these strategies, individuals can gain control over their financial situation, improve their mental and physical health, and inspire others to embark on a similar journey towards financial well-being.

The Dark Reality of Banking: Understanding the Creation of Money

A Poetic Synopsis

"Breaking Free from the Cycle of Financial Fear."

In the shadows of worry, where anxieties bloom,

Lies a path to peace, beyond the gloom.

Mimi, and Zamar found their way,

Through mindful breath and thoughts to sway.

With every breath, they stilled their mind,

Leaving fear and stress behind.

In journals kept, they wrote their plight,

Transforming darkness into light.

Budgets drawn with careful hand,

Turning chaos into planned.

Small steps forward, goals in sight,

Each day bringing newfound might.

Through mindful acts, and thoughts rephrased,

TAI-ZAMARAI YASHARAHYALAH

Their lives transformed, their spirits raised.

From sleepless nights to peaceful dreams,

They broke the cycle, silenced screams.

Their stories tell of hope and grace,

Of finding calm in life's fast pace.

A journey shared, a lesson clear,

In mindful steps, we conquer fear.

Let their tales inspire, ignite,

A path to peace, a beacon bright.

For in each heart, a strength resides,

To turn the tides, and calm the tides.

The Dark Reality of Banking:
Understanding the Creation of Money

Chapter 13

Redefining Value Beyond Money

TAI-ZAMARAI YASHARAHYALAH

The Broader Spectrum of Value Beyond the Pursuit of Wealth

In the relentless pursuit of wealth, it's easy to lose sight of the broader spectrums of value that truly enrich our lives. By redefining what we consider valuable, we can find deeper fulfillment and meaning beyond monetary gains.

This chapter explores the importance of family, community, culture, and spirituality as essential components of a well-rounded and fulfilling life.

Family Values

Family forms the cornerstone of our lives, offering support, love, and a sense of belonging. The intangible benefits of strong family ties often outweigh the financial advantages we seek. Family gatherings, shared experiences, and the unconditional support from loved ones create a foundation of emotional security and happiness that money cannot buy.

Community Values

Communities provide a network of mutual support and cooperation. Being an active member of a community fosters a sense of belonging and purpose. Participation in community activities, local events, and volunteer work enhances social connections and creates a supportive environment where individuals thrive collectively. The value of these relationships often surpasses any financial success.

The Dark Reality of Banking: Understanding the Creation of Money

Cultural Values

Cultural heritage and traditions give us a sense of identity and continuity. They connect us to our past and guide us in the present. Celebrating cultural events, preserving traditions, and passing down stories and customs enrich our lives in profound ways. Cultural values also teach us empathy and respect for diversity, broadening our perspectives and fostering a more inclusive society.

Spiritual Values

Spirituality, whether rooted in religion or personal beliefs, provides a deeper sense of purpose and connection to something greater than ourselves. Spiritual practices, such as meditation, prayer, or mindfulness, offer solace and inner peace. They help us navigate life's challenges with resilience and grace. Spiritual values remind us to focus on the present moment, appreciate the beauty of life, and cultivate gratitude and compassion.

A Poetic Synopsis

"Redefining Value Beyond Money."

In the chase for gold, we often stray,

TAI-ZAMARAI YASHARAHYALAH

From treasures found in life's array.

Beyond the coins, beyond the greed,

Lie values rich, our hearts indeed.

In family's arms, love's sweet embrace,

A warmth no wealth can e'er replace.

Through laughter shared and tears we weep,

In bonds of blood, our souls we keep.

Communities of heart and hand,

Together strong, united stand.

In every face, a friend, a guide,

In shared pursuits, our spirits tied.

Culture's threads, a tapestry,

Of stories told, of history.

In dance and song, traditions flow,

A lineage that helps us grow.

In spiritual realms, we seek and find,

A peace within, a heart aligned.

☐

The Dark Reality of Banking: Understanding the Creation of Money

Through faith and thought, through silent prayer,

We touch the infinite, the rare.

So let us pause and redefine,

What's truly precious, what's divine.

For in the heart, not in the purse,

True wealth resides, a universe.

TAI-ZAMARAI YASHARAHYALAH

The Importance of Non-Monetary Values in Creating a Fulfilling Life

In today's fast-paced world, it's easy to equate success and happiness with financial wealth. However, non-monetary values play a crucial role in creating a truly fulfilling life. These values encompass aspects of our existence that provide deeper satisfaction and meaning beyond material possessions. Recognizing and embracing these values can lead to a more balanced and enriched life.

Emotional Well-being

Emotional well-being is a cornerstone of a fulfilling life. This encompasses a range of factors including mental health, emotional resilience, and the ability to cope with stress. While money can provide temporary relief, true emotional well-being is often rooted in relationships, self-awareness, and personal growth. Activities that promote mental health, such as mindfulness, therapy, and engaging in hobbies, contribute significantly to our overall happiness.

Personal Relationships

Strong personal relationships with family and friends are indispensable for a fulfilling life. These relationships provide emotional support, companionship, and a sense of belonging. Unlike monetary wealth, the richness of personal connections is measured by the quality of interactions and

The Dark Reality of Banking: Understanding the Creation of Money

mutual care. Investing time and effort in nurturing these relationships leads to a deeper sense of fulfillment and joy.

Community Involvement

Active participation in community life fosters a sense of purpose and belonging. Communities offer a support network, opportunities for social interaction, and a chance to contribute to something larger than oneself. Whether through volunteer work, local events, or communal activities, being part of a community enhances our social bonds and reinforces the importance of collective well-being.

Intellectual Growth

Lifelong learning and intellectual curiosity are key components of a fulfilling life. Pursuing knowledge, exploring new ideas, and developing skills not only enrich our minds but also provide a sense of accomplishment and personal growth. Intellectual engagement keeps our minds sharp and opens doors to new experiences and perspectives.

Physical Health

Maintaining good physical health is vital for overall well-being. Regular exercise, a balanced diet, and adequate rest contribute to our physical vitality and longevity. While financial resources can facilitate access to healthcare, the true value lies in daily habits and lifestyle choices that promote health and prevent illness.

Spiritual Fulfillment

Spiritual fulfillment, whether through religious practices or personal beliefs, provides a deeper sense of purpose and inner peace. It encourages us to reflect on our existence, connect with our inner selves, and appreciate the beauty of life. Spiritual practices such as meditation, prayer, or spending time in nature help us cultivate gratitude and compassion, enriching our lives in profound ways.

Cultural and Creative Expression

Engaging in cultural and creative activities allows us to express ourselves and connect with others. Whether through art, music, dance, or literature, creative expression enriches our lives and brings joy. It also fosters a sense of identity and continuity, connecting us to our heritage and the broader human experience.

A Poetic Synopsis

"Embracing Non-Monetary Values."

In the hustle for wealth, we often forget,

The treasures of life we haven't met.

Beyond the shine of gold and greed,

☐

The Dark Reality of Banking: Understanding the Creation of Money

Lie values rich, in hearts they seed.

Emotions warm, a gentle touch,

A mental peace, we crave so much.

In mindfulness, our spirits find,

A solace deep, a quiet mind.

In family's arms, where love resides,

A bond so strong, where heart confides.

Through joy and sorrow, day and night,

In kinship's glow, we find our light.

Communities where hearts unite,

In shared pursuits, we find delight.

A network strong, a helping hand,

Together firm, we proudly stand.

In knowledge vast, our minds expand,

A journey rich, so finely planned.

Through books and thoughts, and skills anew,

TAI-ZAMARAI YASHARAHYALAH

Our intellect, it thrives and grew.

Health of body, health of soul,

In wellness true, we find our goal.

With every step, in nature's grace,

We nurture life, at gentle pace.

In spirit's quest, we seek and find,

A peace within, a heart aligned.

Through prayer and thought, through sacred air,

We touch the infinite, the rare.

In art and song, in dance and play,

Our spirits soar, in light array.

In culture's fold, our roots we trace,

A heritage, a warm embrace.

So let us pause and redefine,

What's truly precious, what's divine.

For in the heart, not in the purse,

True wealth resides, a universe.

Practical Steps to Integrate Diverse Values into Daily Living

Incorporating diverse values into our daily lives can profoundly enrich our experience and lead to a more balanced and fulfilling existence. Here are practical steps to help integrate emotional well-being, personal relationships, community involvement, intellectual growth, physical health, spiritual fulfillment, and cultural and creative expression into daily living:

Emotional Well-being

1. *Practice Mindfulness and Meditation*: Set aside time each day for mindfulness or meditation to reduce stress and increase self-awareness.

2. *Journaling*: Write down your thoughts, feelings, and experiences regularly to process emotions and reflect on your mental state.

3. *Seek Professional Help*: Don't hesitate to seek therapy or counseling if you need support with emotional challenges.

Personal Relationships

1. *Schedule Quality Time*: Dedicate specific times in your week to spend with family and friends, ensuring uninterrupted, meaningful interaction.

2. *Express Appreciation*: Regularly show gratitude and appreciation for your loved ones through words and actions.

3. *Active Listening*: Practice active listening by giving full attention, acknowledging feelings, and responding thoughtfully during conversations.

Community Involvement

1. *Volunteer*: Find local organizations or causes that resonate with your values and beliefs and commit to building with them as regularly as you can.

2. *Attend Community Events:* Participate in community gatherings, events, and activities to strengthen your connection with your local community.

3. *Support Local Initiatives*: Engage in and support local businesses, farmers' markets, and community projects.

Intellectual Growth

1. *Lifelong Learning*: Enroll in courses, workshops, or online classes to continuously expand your knowledge and skills.

2. *Read Regularly*: Make reading a daily habit. Choose books, articles, and publications that challenge, inspire, and sharpen you.

3. *Cultivate Curiosity:* Embrace a curious mindset by exploring new topics, asking questions, and seeking diverse perspectives.

Physical Health

1. *Exercise Regularly*: Incorporate physical activity into your daily routine, whether it's through gym workouts, Tai-Chi, walking, or sports.

2. *Healthy Eating*: Plan balanced meals and prioritize whole, nutritious foods while minimizing processed foods.

3. *Adequate Rest*: Ensure you get enough sleep each night and take breaks throughout the day to rest and recharge.

Spiritual Fulfillment

1. *Daily Reflection:* Spend time each day in reflection, prayer, or meditation to connect with your inner Chi (inner self) and values.

2. *Nature Connection:* Spend time in nature to find peace and gain perspective, appreciating the beauty and tranquility around you.

3. *Gratitude Practice*: Keep a gratitude journal to regularly note things you are thankful for, fostering a sense of contentment and spiritual richness.

Cultural and Creative Expression

1. *Engage in the Arts*: Participate in artistic activities such as painting, writing, music, or dance to express yourself creatively. This helps boost your confidence, self awareness and self esteem.

2. *Cultural Exploration*: Explore different cultures through travel, language learning, and cultural events to broaden your horizons.

3. *Support the Arts*: Attend performances, exhibitions, and cultural festivals to immerse yourself in the creative works of others in your world and support local artists.

A Poetic Synopsis

"Integrating Diverse Values into Daily Living."

In every dawn, a chance to blend,

Life's values deep, around the bend.

Not just in coins or fleeting fame,

But in the heart, where life's aflame.

In quiet moments, find your peace,

☐

The Dark Reality of Banking: Understanding the Creation of Money

Let mindfulness, your stress release.

With journal's ink, emotions pour,

In written lines, your spirit soar.

In family's warmth, your time invest,

In love and care, you'll find your rest.

With friends, in joy and sorrow share,

In every bond, feel hearts repair.

Engage your community, lend a hand,

In unity, together stand.

At local events, your presence show,

In shared pursuits, your friendships grow.

Let books and learning feed your mind,

In every page, new worlds you'll find.

Stay curious, let questions lead,

In knowledge vast, your spirit freed.

Keep body strong, in health's embrace,

TAI-ZAMARAI YASHARAHYALAH

With exercise, life's challenges face.

In wholesome meals, find nature's wealth,

In rest, restore your inner health.

In quiet reflection, seek the light,

In spiritual calm, your heart ignite.

In nature's arms, find solace sweet,

In gratitude, your soul complete.

In art and culture, joy express,

In every stroke, your heart confess.

Explore the world, its wonders trace,

In every culture, find your place.

So weave these values in your day,

In every act, let them convey.

A life enriched, beyond the gold,

In heart and soul, true wealth behold.

The Dark Reality of Banking:
Understanding the Creation of Money

Chapter 14

Creating a Balanced Approach to Financial and Personal Well-Being

TAI-ZAMARAI YASHARAHYALAH

Combining Sound Financial Planning with Holistic Well-Being

In today's fast-paced world, achieving a balance between financial stability and personal well-being is crucial. This chapter explores how combining sound financial planning with holistic well-being practices can lead to a more fulfilling and resilient life.

Combining Financial Planning with Holistic Well-being Practices

1. Financial Planning for Security and Peace of Mind

1. *Budgeting and Saving*: Create a detailed budget that includes all sources of income and expenses. Prioritize saving by setting aside a portion of your income for emergencies and future goals.

2. *Debt Management:* Develop a strategy to pay off existing debts while avoiding accumulating new ones. Consider consolidating debts to simplify payments and reduce interest rates.

3. *Investment:* Educate yourself on investment options and seek advice from financial professionals to grow your wealth sustainably. Diversify your investments to mitigate risks.

2. Integrating Well-being Practices for a Balanced Life

1. *Physical Health:* Incorporate regular exercise and healthy eating habits into your routine. Physical well-being supports mental clarity and emotional stability.

2. *Mental Health:* Practice mindfulness, meditation, and stress-reducing activities. Prioritize mental health through regular self-care and, if necessary, professional counseling.

3. *Social Connections*: Foster meaningful relationships with family, friends, and the community. Social support is essential for emotional well-being and can provide a sense of belonging and purpose.

3. Creating a Synergistic Approach

1. *Align Financial Goals with Personal Values*: Ensure that your financial goals reflect your personal values and long-term aspirations. For example, if family is a priority, allocate resources for family activities and education.

2. *Mindful Spending*: Make conscious decisions about spending. Prioritize experiences and purchases that enhance your overall well-being rather than impulsive or status-driven buys.

3. *Work-Life Balance*: Strive for a balance between professional responsibilities and personal time. Set boundaries to protect personal time from work demands and invest time in activities that rejuvenate you.

4. Tools and Techniques for a Balanced Approach

1. *Financial Wellness Programs*: Many employers offer financial wellness programs that provide education and resources to help employees manage their finances. Take advantage of these programs to improve your financial literacy and planning skills.

2. *Holistic Health Resources*: Utilize resources such as wellness apps, online courses, and community programs that promote a holistic approach to health. These can provide guidance and support in maintaining balance.

3. *Goal Setting and Tracking*: Use tools like vision boards, journals, or digital apps to set, track, and review both financial and personal well-being goals. Regularly revisiting these goals can help maintain focus and motivation.

5. Overcoming Challenges and Building Resilience

1. *Adaptability:* Be prepared to adapt your financial and well-being strategies as life circumstances change. Flexibility is key to maintaining balance during transitions and unexpected events.

2. *Building a Support Network:* Surround yourself with supportive individuals who understand and respect your

goals. Seek advice and encouragement from mentors, peers, and professional advisors.

3. *Continuous Learning*: Stay informed about financial trends and well-being practices. Continuous learning helps you make informed decisions and adapt to new challenges.

A Poetic Synopsis

"Creating a Balanced Approach to Financial and Personal Well-being."

In life's grand dance, seek balance true,

Not just in gold, but in all you pursue.

With budgeting wise, and savings clear,

Financial peace will draw near.

Debt's heavy chains, cast them away,

Invest with wisdom, for a brighter day.

But wealth alone, does not define,

A life well-lived, with joy entwined.

TAI-ZAMARAI YASHARAHYALAH

In health's embrace, both mind and form,

Find strength and calm, through every storm.

With friends and kin, in laughter share,

In love's warm glow, life's burdens bear.

Align your goals, with values dear,

Spend mindfully, let purpose steer.

Balance work, with restful play,

In harmony, your spirit stay.

Tools and guides, at your command,

To plan, to track, to understand.

In challenges, find strength anew,

With resilience, see them through.

For in this blend, of coin and care,

A richer life, beyond compare.

In balanced stride, your path unfurl,

A life of worth, a precious pearl.

Developing a Balanced Mindset Toward Money and Life

In the pursuit of a harmonious life, developing a balanced mindset toward money and other aspects of existence is essential. This chapter delves into practical strategies and philosophical approaches to achieving equilibrium between financial pursuits and personal fulfillment.

Understanding the Interplay Between Money and Life

1. The Role of Money

1. Tool for Security: Recognize money as a tool that provides security and meets basic needs. It is a means to an end, not an end in itself.

2. Facilitator of Experiences: Use money to create memorable experiences and enrich life rather than accumulating it for status or power.

3. Enabler of Contributions: Leverage financial resources to contribute to societal good and support causes that align with your values.

2. The Role of Life Values

1. *Identifying Core Values*: Reflect on what matters most to you—family, health, education, community, and personal growth. These values should guide your financial decisions.

2. *Life Beyond Wealth*: Understand that true fulfillment comes from a balanced life that includes relationships, personal achievements, and self-improvement, not just financial success.

Practical Strategies for a Balanced Mindset

1. Mindful Financial Management

1. Budget with Purpose: Create a budget that reflects your values and priorities. Allocate funds for essentials, savings, experiences, and giving back.

2. Mindful Spending: Before making purchases, consider if they align with your long-term goals and values. Avoid impulsive buying driven by emotions or societal pressure.

3. Saving and Investing Wisely: Develop a savings plan and invest in opportunities that align with your values and provide long-term security.

2. Cultivating Personal Well-being

1. Health and Wellness: Invest time and resources in maintaining your physical and mental health. Regular exercise, balanced nutrition, and mental health practices like meditation contribute to overall well-being.

2. *Work-Life Balance:* Set boundaries to ensure work does not encroach on personal time. Prioritize activities that rejuvenate and inspire you.

3. *Continuous Learning*: Embrace lifelong learning to grow personally and professionally. This can lead to better financial decision-making and personal satisfaction.

3. Building Meaningful Relationships

1. *Quality Time with Loved Ones:* Spend quality time with family and friends. These relationships provide emotional support and enrich life experiences.

2. *Community Engagement:* Participate in community activities and volunteer work. Contributing to the well-being of others fosters a sense of purpose and connection.

4. Embracing a Growth Mindset

1. *Adapting to Change:* Accept that change is a constant part of life. Flexibility and a willingness to adapt can help you navigate financial and personal challenges.

2. *Resilience and Positivity*: Cultivate resilience by maintaining a positive outlook and focusing on solutions rather than problems. This mindset helps in overcoming setbacks and finding opportunities in adversity.

Philosophical Approaches to Balance

1. The Concept of Enough

1. Defining Enough: Understand what "enough" means for you. This includes financial stability, fulfilling relationships, and personal growth.

2. Contentment and Gratitude: Practice gratitude for what you have rather than constantly striving for more. Contentment is key to a balanced life.

2. Integrating Financial Goals with Life Aspirations

1. Holistic Goal Setting: Set goals that encompass both financial and personal aspirations. Ensure they are aligned and mutually supportive.

2. Regular Reflection and Adjustment: Periodically review and adjust your goals and strategies to ensure they continue to align with your evolving values and circumstances.

The Dark Reality of Banking: Understanding the Creation of Money

A Poetic Synopsis

"Developing a Balanced Mindset Toward Money and Life."

In the dance of life, with steps so fine,

Money's role, let's now define.

A tool it is, for needs and dreams,

Not the end, but means it seems.

Reflect on values, heart held dear,

Let them guide your path, so clear.

From health to love, and learning's light,

Find balance in both day and night.

With budget wise and spending kind,

In every choice, let purpose find.

Save and invest, with future in view,

For security and dreams, anew.

TAI-ZAMARAI YASHARAHYALAH

In health and joy, invest your time,

In work and play, find rhythm's rhyme.

With loved ones near, and community strong,

In their embrace, you'll find where you belong.

Embrace the change, with open heart,

Adapt and grow, as life imparts.

Resilience build, with hope so bright,

In every storm, find guiding light.

Define what's enough, in life's embrace,

With gratitude, find your place.

Goals aligned, both near and far,

Balance found, like guiding star.

In harmony of wealth and soul,

A life complete, a spirit whole.

For in this dance, of joy and strife,

Find balance true, in money and life.

Building a Sustainable Future with Financial and Personal Harmony

In today's fast-paced world, achieving sustainability extends beyond environmental concerns—it encompasses financial stability and personal well-being. This chapter explores the interconnectedness of financial practices and personal values, guiding readers toward a future where economic and personal growth harmoniously coexist.

The Essence of Sustainability

1. Defining Sustainability

1. Environmental: Ensuring that our actions today do not deplete resources or harm the planet, preserving it for future generations.

2. Financial: Establishing a stable financial foundation that supports long-term goals and withstands economic fluctuations.

3. Personal: Maintaining a lifestyle that nurtures physical, mental, and emotional health, promoting overall well-being.

Principles of Financial Sustainability

1. Responsible Spending and Saving

1. Budgeting for Balance: Create a budget that covers essentials, savings, and discretionary spending, ensuring all aspects of life are funded appropriately.

2. Debt Management: Prioritize paying off high-interest debt and avoid accumulating new debt. Practice responsible borrowing.

3. Emergency Fund: Establish an emergency fund to cover unforeseen expenses, providing financial security and peace of mind.

2. Ethical Investing

1. Sustainable Investments: Choose investments that align with environmental, social, and governance (ESG) criteria, supporting companies that prioritize sustainability.

2. Long-Term Focus: Invest with a long-term perspective, considering the impact of investments on future generations.

3. Financial Education

1. Continuous Learning: Stay informed about financial markets, investment strategies, and personal finance management.

2. *Financial Literacy:* Educate yourself and others about financial principles, empowering informed decision-making.

Principles of Personal Harmony

1. Health and Wellness

1. Physical Health: Prioritize regular exercise, balanced nutrition, and sufficient rest to maintain optimal physical health.

2. Mental Health: Practice mindfulness, meditation, and stress management techniques to support mental well-being.

3. Emotional Health: Foster positive relationships and engage in activities that bring joy and fulfillment.

2. Work-Life Balance

1. Time Management: Allocate time effectively between work, family, hobbies, and self-care to avoid burnout.

2. Setting Boundaries: Establish clear boundaries to ensure personal time is protected and respected.

3. Community and Relationships

1. Community Involvement: Participate in community

activities and volunteer work, contributing to societal well-being and creating a sense of belonging.

2. *Nurturing Relationships:* Invest time and effort in building and maintaining meaningful relationships with family and friends.

Integrating Financial and Personal Harmony

1. Aligning Financial Goals with Personal Values

1. Value-Based Budgeting: Ensure your budget reflects your personal values, funding activities and causes that are important to you.

2. Purposeful Spending: Make purchasing decisions that enhance your quality of life and align with your long-term goals.

2. Holistic Financial Planning

1. Comprehensive Approach: Develop a financial plan that incorporates all aspects of life, including retirement, healthcare, education, and personal aspirations.

2. Regular Review: Periodically review and adjust your financial plan to stay aligned with changing circumstances and evolving values.

3. Sustainable Lifestyle Choices

The Dark Reality of Banking: Understanding the Creation of Money

1. *Minimalism:* Adopt a minimalist approach to consumption, focusing on quality over quantity and reducing waste.

2. *Eco-Friendly Practices:* Incorporate environmentally friendly habits into daily life, such as reducing energy consumption, recycling, and supporting sustainable products.

A Poetic Synopsis

"Building a Sustainable Future with Financial and Personal Harmony."

In a world where futures intertwine,

Sustainability's the design.

Not just the earth, but wealth and soul,

In harmony, we find our goal.

Budget wise, for needs and dreams,

In balance, spend—so it seems.

Debt in check, savings secure,

TAI-ZAMARAI YASHARAHYALAH

Financial peace, foundation sure.

Invest with heart, in futures bright,

Where ethics meet the market's might.

Long-term vision, wise and clear,

For generations, we hold dear.

Health in body, mind, and heart,

In wellness, find the perfect start.

Exercise, rest, and mindful care,

In balance found, joy's always there.

Work and life, in perfect blend,

Time for self, and time to lend.

Boundaries set, and managed well,

In this dance, we break the spell.

Community, where roots run deep,

In giving, find the peace we seek.

Relationships, both strong and true,

In love and care, our strength renew.

The Dark Reality of Banking: Understanding the Creation of Money

Financial goals, with values tied,

In purposeful paths, we stride.

Holistic plans, for life's vast span,

Adjust and grow, as seasons can.

Minimalism, in life embraced,

Quality over waste replaced.

Eco habits, day by day,

In every choice, a better way.

In harmony of wealth and being,

A sustainable future, clearly seeing.

For in this blend, we find the key,

To live in peace and prosperity.

TAI-ZAMARAI YASHARAHYALAH

Supplementary Chapter

The Dystopian Future of Central Bank Digital Currencies

The Dark Reality of Banking: Understanding the Creation of Money

A Discussion with an Economist

Interviewer: We'll be discussing CBDCs primarily. In this day and age, economics seems more emotional and political than ever before. What are your thoughts?

Economist: Exactly. The reality is, of course, that economics is always about money and power. That's precisely why the mainstream has neither money nor power in their models. There's not even money in these economic models, certainly not banks either. And power is considered off-limits.

When the 2008 banking crisis happened, journalists wanted to interview experts. They asked professors of economics at Harvard, MIT, Oxford to comment on the banks going bust, stock markets collapsing, companies failing, and the economy shrinking. The honest answer from these professors should have been, "Sorry, I can't comment." Why? Because their models don't include banks. And this is still true for most central banks today, using these dynamic stochastic general equilibrium models. They assume a fictional world of equilibrium, which is highly unrealistic.

Interviewer: And what about the implications of Central Bank Digital Currencies (CBDCs)?

Economist: If CBDCs are introduced, it will lead to a Soviet-style economy. Central Bank Digital Currencies are a misnomer, designed to confuse people with the acronym CBDC, suggesting the digital aspect is new. We've been using BDCs, bank digital currencies, for decades. The digital aspect is nothing new; it's the centralization that's new.

Interviewer: So, if CBDCs are inevitable, how will it end in the long run?

Economist: It will lead to a completely dystopian scenario within a decade. It's so dire that we should stop it in its tracks and not even allow pilot projects.

Interviewer: But isn't economics about more than just transactions? What about the balance of power, especially with the introduction of CBDCs?

Economist: Economics, at its core, is about money and power. In reality, we don't have equilibrium; we have rationing. Rationing means demand is not equal to supply in every market. The short side principle applies, meaning the smaller quantity of demand or supply determines the outcome. The short side has power, and power is in every market. This fundamental tool, money, shows that the short side is the supply of money.

Most people think the government or the central bank creates the majority of the money supply, but that's not true. Governments create zero money; they borrow money at interest. Central banks create only about 3-4% of the money supply. The banks create the remaining 97%. Banks don't take deposits; they don't lend money. They purchase securities. When you take a loan, you're essentially issuing a

The Dark Reality of Banking: Understanding the Creation of Money

promissory note that the bank buys. The bank creates a deposit, which is just a record of its debt to you.

Interviewer: So, how does this process change with CBDCs?

Economist: The introduction of CBDCs will centralize the creation and control of money, effectively turning central banks into the main player in the economy. This centralization is dangerous and reminiscent of a Soviet-style economy. The central planners will argue for more power, claiming they need it to stabilize the economy, but this will only lead to more control and less freedom.

Interviewer: Isn't there an argument that creative destruction through boom and bust cycles spurs innovation?

Economist: Innovation and creativity happen without the destructive resource misallocation and waste from boom-bust cycles. The East Asian high-growth economies, like Japan, Korea, Taiwan, and China, have shown that you can have sustained double-digit economic growth by ensuring bank credit is used for productive business investment. This increases productivity and value, leading to higher economic growth without the inefficiencies of boom-bust cycles.

Interviewer: So, in summary, what's the future with CBDCs?

Economist: If we allow CBDCs, we will move towards a

highly centralized, controlled economy. The centralization aspect of CBDCs is the real danger, not the digital aspect. Central Bank Digital Currencies will lead to an unprecedented level of control over the economy, stifling innovation, and individual freedom, ultimately resulting in a dystopian, Soviet-style economic system.

A Song of the Central Bank Digital Currency (CBDC)

In the age of screens and digital streams,

A new dawn rises, or so it seems.

Beyond the coins and paper notes,

A currency floats on cyber boats.

Central Bank Digital Currency born,

From finance's ancient cloak, it's torn.

Promises bright of ease and grace,

In virtual vaults, it finds its place.

No jingling coins, no crumpled bills,

Just data streams through coded hills.

The Dark Reality of Banking: Understanding the Creation of Money

Transactions swift as lightning's flight,

In CBDC's electric light.

Yet shadows lurk in this bright realm,

With central hands upon the helm.

Privacy fades, replaced by sight,

Of every move in day and night.

Control so tight, can freedom sing,

When every spend reports to king?

In whispers soft, concerns arise,

Of power's grip and freedom's ties.

The banker's dream, the technocrat's glee,

A new form of currency, we see.

Transparent chains in blockchain's weave,

But do they grant, or just deceive?

Efficiency, the new coin's grace,

Yet what of liberty's embrace?

TAI-ZAMARAI YASHARAHYALAH

In digital we trust and fear,

A future bright, yet shadowed near.

So, ponder well this path we tread,

In the world of CBDC ahead.

For in its glow and promise sweet,

Lie questions deep of what's complete.

Will we embrace this currency new,

With cautious steps and insights true?

Or will we find our freedoms sold,

For digital chains of gleaming gold?

In balance, wisdom, we must seek,

As future paths of finance speak.

For every gain in tech's delight,

Let's guard the values held in sight.

Cashless Keys to Success

A Holistic Exploration

In a rapidly evolving world, the traditional metrics of success—often tied to financial wealth—are being redefined. Success today is a multifaceted concept that encompasses a variety of elements beyond monetary gain. By exploring these diverse dimensions, we can develop a more holistic understanding of what it means to truly succeed in life.

Personal Fulfillment

Success begins with personal fulfillment, which includes pursuing passions, developing talents, and achieving personal goals. It's about finding joy in what you do and continuously striving for self-improvement. When individuals align their careers and personal lives with their intrinsic interests, they achieve a sense of purpose and satisfaction that transcends financial rewards.

Health and Well-being

Good health is a cornerstone of success. Physical, mental, and emotional well-being are essential for sustaining long-term achievements. Regular exercise, a balanced diet, mindfulness practices, and adequate rest are crucial. Mental health, often neglected in traditional success paradigms, is equally important. The ability to manage stress, maintain emotional balance, and cultivate resilience plays a significant role in achieving and maintaining success.

Relationships and Community

Success is deeply rooted in the quality of our relationships. Building and nurturing connections with family, friends, colleagues, and the broader community provides emotional support, opportunities for collaboration, and a sense of belonging. Strong relationships contribute to personal happiness and professional growth, emphasizing the value of empathy, communication, and mutual respect.

Contribution and Impact

True success extends beyond personal gain to include the positive impact one has on society. This can manifest through community service, environmental stewardship, mentoring, or creating products and services that improve lives. Contributing to the greater good fosters a sense of pride and fulfillment, reinforcing the idea that success is not solely about accumulation but also about giving back.

Financial Stability

While not the sole determinant of success, financial stability provides the freedom to pursue other dimensions of a successful life. It involves prudent management of resources, savings, and investments to ensure security and opportunities for future endeavors. Financial success should be viewed as a means to support overall well-being rather than an end in itself.

Lifelong Learning

Continuous education and personal development are crucial for sustained success. The world is constantly changing, and staying curious and open to learning new skills and perspectives is vital. This mindset fosters adaptability and innovation, allowing individuals to navigate challenges and seize new opportunities.

Spiritual and Ethical Integrity

For many, spiritual beliefs and ethical principles are a guiding force and provide a foundation in their pursuit of success. Living in accordance with one's values, whether they are derived from culture, philosophy, or personal convictions, adds a dimension of integrity and authenticity. This alignment can guide decisions and actions, ensuring that success is achieved in a manner that is both fulfilling and morally sound.

Spiritual fulfillment, whether through cultural practices, meditation, or a connection to nature, adds a profound dimension to success. It involves seeking deeper meaning and purpose in life, aligning actions with core beliefs, and nurturing the inner self. Success here is about being true to one's values and ensuring that actions and decisions align with a higher moral or spiritual code. This brings inner peace, resilience, and a sense of interconnectedness.

Success is a complex and dynamic concept that cannot be measured by financial wealth alone. It encompasses personal fulfillment, health, relationships, societal impact, financial stability, lifelong learning, balance, and ethical integrity. By embracing this holistic approach, individuals can pursue a more meaningful and sustainable form of success, one that enriches not only their own lives but also the lives of those around them. In a cashless society, these values become the true currency, fostering a richer, more connected, and fulfilling human experience.

Expanding the Dimensions

In an age where the meaning of success is continually evolving, it's essential to understand that true success transcends financial wealth. To fully grasp the breadth of success, we must explore its various dimensions that encompass personal growth, community involvement, and ethical living.

Health and Well-being

Physical and mental health are fundamental to any notion of success. Maintaining a healthy lifestyle through balanced nutrition, regular exercise, and mental health practices ensures the energy and clarity needed to pursue goals. Emotional well-being, often overlooked, is crucial; it involves cultivating positive relationships, managing stress, and seeking support when needed.

Health and wellness are critical to achieving and maintaining success. Success means prioritizing self-care, managing stress effectively, and maintaining a healthy work-life balance to ensure long-term vitality and productivity.

The Dark Reality of Banking: Understanding the Creation of Money

Relationships and Community

Strong, supportive relationships form a critical component of success. Building and maintaining connections with family, friends, and the community fosters a network of support and shared resources. Success in this context means being an active participant in your community, offering and receiving support, and contributing to the well-being of others.

Community engagement and service play a vital role in a fulfilling life. Success includes actively participating in and contributing to your community, whether through volunteer work, local initiatives, or supporting causes you care about. This fosters a sense of belonging, purpose, and shared responsibility, enhancing both personal fulfillment and communal well-being.

Resilient relationships are the foundation of a successful and happy life. This includes cultivating strong, supportive connections with family, friends, and colleagues. Success means nurturing these relationships through empathy, communication, and mutual respect, which provides a support system during both good and challenging times.

Contribution and Impact

True success includes making a positive impact on the world. This might involve volunteer work, philanthropic efforts, or simply being a positive influence in your daily interactions. Success here is measured by the difference one makes in the lives of others and in their community, reflecting a commitment to something greater than oneself.

Balance and Harmony

Achieving balance is essential for sustainable success. This means ensuring that different aspects of life, such as work, family, health, and leisure, are given appropriate attention. Balance prevents burnout and ensures a holistic approach to success, where no single area dominates at the expense of others.

A harmonious life prevents burnout and ensures that no single area is neglected. Time management, setting priorities, and creating boundaries are key strategies for maintaining balance.

Sustainability and Environmental Stewardship

Incorporating sustainability and environmental responsibility into the concept of success is increasingly important. This involves making choices that reduce environmental impact, supporting sustainable practices, and considering the long-term health of the planet. Success means contributing to a future where both people and nature can thrive.

Environmental stewardship is increasingly recognized as an integral part of success. This involves making sustainable choices that reduce environmental impact, advocating for policies that protect the planet, and educating others about environmental issues. Success means living in harmony with nature and contributing to the preservation of the Earth for future generations.

The Dark Reality of Banking: Understanding the Creation of Money

Technological Savvy and Adaptation

In our digital age, being technologically savvy is a crucial part of success. Understanding and leveraging technology can enhance personal and professional life. However, success also involves being mindful of technology's impact on mental health and personal relationships, ensuring its use is balanced and purposeful.

In an increasingly digital world, success involves staying informed about technological advancements, leveraging digital tools to enhance productivity and connectivity, and understanding the ethical implications of technology. This ensures you remain competitive and relevant in both personal and professional spheres.

True success is a multi-dimensional concept that goes far beyond financial achievement. It encompasses personal fulfillment, health, relationships, societal impact, financial stability, lifelong learning, balance, ethical living, sustainability, and technological adaptation. By adopting a holistic approach to success, individuals can lead richer, more meaningful lives that contribute positively to their communities and the world. This comprehensive view allows for a sustainable, fulfilling path to success that values the well-being of all, rather than just the accumulation of wealth.

Lifelong Learning and Growth

Lifelong learning and growth are fundamental to sustained success. This involves continuously seeking knowledge, developing new skills, and staying curious about the world. Success means embracing a mindset of constant improvement and being open to new experiences and ideas, which helps to stay relevant and adaptable and enables individuals to innovate, overcome challenges, as well as capitalize on opportunities. in a rapidly changing world.

Innovation in Personal and Professional Life

Innovation should not be confined to the workplace; it is equally important in personal life. This means approaching personal challenges with creativity and open-mindedness, finding new ways to solve problems, and continuously improving your lifestyle. In professional life, innovation drives growth, efficiency, and competitive advantage.

Personal fulfillment lies at the heart of success. It's about engaging in activities that bring joy and satisfaction, whether through creative pursuits, professional achievements, or personal hobbies. Success in this realm means aligning one's actions with their passions and values, leading to a profound sense of purpose and happiness.

Purpose-Driven Life

Living a purpose-driven life aligns actions and decisions with your core values and long-term goals. Success means having a clear sense of purpose that guides your life choices, providing motivation and fulfillment. This purpose often extends beyond personal achievement to include contributing to the greater good and making a positive impact.

The Dark Reality of Banking:
Understanding the Creation of Money

Cultural and Intellectual Enrichment

Cultural and intellectual enrichment adds depth and richness to life. Success means engaging with diverse cultural experiences, appreciating the arts, and pursuing intellectual interests. This broadens perspectives, fosters creativity, and enhances personal growth and empathy.

Mentorship and Legacy Building

Mentorship and legacy building are powerful ways to achieve lasting success. Success means sharing your knowledge and experience with others, mentoring the next generation, and building a legacy that reflects your values and contributions. This creates a ripple effect, influencing others positively long after your direct involvement.

Holistic Integration

Holistic integration involves blending all these elements into a cohesive approach to life. Success means balancing different aspects of well-being, personal growth, and societal impact in a way that is harmonious and sustainable. This integrated approach ensures a well-rounded, fulfilling, and impactful life journey.

True success is a multifaceted, dynamic concept that goes beyond financial achievements. It encompasses personal fulfillment, health, meaningful relationships, community involvement, and a positive impact on the world. By embracing a holistic view of success, individuals can create a balanced, enriching, and sustainable life that benefits themselves and those around them. This comprehensive approach encourages ongoing growth, adaptability, and a deep sense of purpose, leading to a truly successful and fulfilling existence.

Mindfulness and Presence

Mindfulness and presence are crucial in our fast-paced world. Success involves being fully engaged in the present moment, appreciating the here and now, and reducing distractions. This practice enhances mental clarity, reduces stress, and improves relationships by fostering deeper connections and a more focused approach to life and work.

Resilience and Adaptability

Resilience and adaptability are essential traits for navigating life's inevitable ups and downs. Success means being able to bounce back from setbacks, learn from failures, and adapt to changing circumstances. Cultivating a growth mindset, where challenges are viewed as opportunities for learning and growth, is key to long-term success.

Innovation and Creativity

Innovation and creativity drive progress and personal fulfillment. Success in this area means thinking outside the box, embracing new ideas, and being willing to take risks. It's about finding unique solutions to problems and continually seeking ways to improve and evolve, both personally and professionally.

Gratitude and Contentment

Gratitude and contentment are often overlooked aspects of success. Appreciating what you have and finding contentment in your current circumstances fosters a positive outlook and emotional well-being. Success means recognizing and celebrating small victories, maintaining a sense of gratitude, and not constantly striving for more at the expense of present happiness.

Time Management and Prioritization

Effective time management and prioritization are critical to achieving success. This involves setting clear goals, managing time efficiently, and prioritizing tasks that align with your values and long-term objectives. Success means focusing on what truly matters and using time wisely to create a balanced and fulfilling life.

Leadership and Influence

Leadership and influence extend beyond formal positions of power. Success in this context involves inspiring and motivating others, leading by example, and making a positive impact through your actions and decisions. Whether in personal, professional, or community settings, strong leadership fosters collaboration, innovation, and positive change.

Ethical Entrepreneurship

Ethical entrepreneurship is about creating value through businesses and ventures that uphold ethical standards and contribute positively to society. Success means building enterprises that are not only profitable but also socially responsible, environmentally sustainable, and aligned with the greater good.

Cultural Awareness and Inclusion

In our diverse world, cultural awareness and inclusion are vital components of success. This involves understanding, respecting, and valuing different cultures and perspectives. Success means fostering inclusive environments where everyone feels valued and respected, which enhances collaboration, creativity, and mutual understanding.

Legacy and Long-term Vision

Thinking about legacy and long-term vision encourages a broader perspective on success. This involves considering the impact of your actions on future generations and striving to leave a positive mark on the world. Success means building a lasting legacy that reflects your values, contributions, and the positive changes you've made.

Holistic Financial Planning

Holistic financial planning integrates financial stability with broader life goals and values. This approach considers not just wealth accumulation, but also how financial resources can support personal growth, family well-being, community involvement, and long-term security. Success means having a comprehensive financial plan that aligns with your life purpose and goals.

The Dark Reality of Banking: Understanding the Creation of Money

Financial stability remains an important aspect of success but should be viewed as a means to support other dimensions of life. Effective money management, savings, and investments are tools that provide security and freedom, allowing individuals to focus on personal and community goals without the constant pressure of financial insecurity.

Global Citizenship

Global citizenship involves recognizing our interconnectedness and taking responsibility for global challenges. Success in this realm means contributing to solutions for global issues such as poverty, climate change, and inequality. It involves understanding the impact of your actions on a global scale and striving to make a positive difference.

Success is a multifaceted journey that encompasses far more than financial wealth. It involves personal fulfillment, health and well-being, strong relationships, community impact, ethical living, and a balanced, holistic approach to life. By embracing these diverse dimensions of success, individuals can lead richer, more meaningful lives that contribute positively to their communities and the world. This comprehensive perspective on success encourages a sustainable, fulfilling path that values well-being, ethical behavior, and global responsibility.

TAI-ZAMARAI YASHARAHYALAH

A Poetic Synopsis

"Cashless Keys to Success."

In the dance of time and fleeting days,

Success is more than golden praise.

It's the lifelong quest for growth and light,

A heart that learns both day and night.

Health and wellness, body and mind,

The balanced life, a treasure to find.

Care for self in every season,

The roots of joy, the core of reason.

To the community, lend your hand,

In service, let your spirit expand.

Find your purpose in deeds and care,

A tapestry of love to share.

Spiritual paths, diverse and true,

Guide the soul with a clearer view.

☐

The Dark Reality of Banking: Understanding the Creation of Money

In nature's calm or sacred halls,

The peace within that never stalls.

Steward the Earth, our fragile home,

In every choice, let kindness roam.

A legacy of green and blue,

For those unborn, a world anew.

Relationships, resilient and strong,

Are melodies in life's sweet song.

In trust and love, we find our way,

A network bright, a warm array.

Innovation's spark, both grand and small,

In every life, let ideas sprawl.

Creativity, the heart's delight,

Transforms the mundane into bright.

Purpose-driven, the path is clear,

Goals aligned, both far and near.

TAI-ZAMARAI YASHARAHYALAH

A compass true, a guiding star,

Leads to places wide and far.

Tech-savvy minds in a digital age,

Navigate change with wisdom sage.

Ethical, sharp, in every task,

In future's face, no questions ask.

Cultural quests and intellectual rise,

Broaden horizons, open eyes.

The arts and thoughts, a vibrant spree,

Expand the heart's capacity.

Mentor, teach, and build your name,

Legacy shines in the hall of fame.

Pass on wisdom, share the light,

In others' growth, our spirits ignite.

Holistic life, a balanced blend,

Success's journey, without end.

In every sphere, a story spun,

The Dark Reality of Banking: Understanding the Creation of Money

A life well-lived, a victory won.

Success, a symphony of parts,

In every beat, the rhythm starts.

Not just wealth, but joy and grace,

In every moment, find your place.

A holistic path, where values thrive,

In this dance, we truly arrive.

Embrace the whole, the broad, the true,

In every step, success renews.

Has the UK Got a Finance Caste?

I feel as like this is a trick question because first off, the uk doesn't have finance.

The city of London is private, has not, and is not part of the UK.

The city of london is outside the United Kingdom (I know that it's really shocking!), and therefore it's also not part of the EU (It couldn't be part of the EU because you'll have to have democratic elections and the city of london doesn't, right?)

When you start unpicking this puzzle it rapidly becomes evident that this is a very dangerous piece of information—an extremely dangerous game because of its implications.

Also, it's not part of the UK because the queen is not allowed to enter without permission—she's not the sovereign

The concept of a "finance caste" refers to a distinct and influential group within society that holds significant power and privilege due to their control over financial resources and institutions. This group often enjoys advantages in terms of wealth, influence, and opportunities that are not accessible to the general population. In examining whether the UK has a finance caste, several factors must be considered: the concentration of financial power, the social and economic mobility within the sector, and the influence of financial elites on policy and society.

1. Concentration of Financial Power:

The UK's financial sector is one of the most significant in the world, particularly centered in the City of London. This area is home to numerous global banks, investment firms, hedge funds, and other financial institutions. A small number of key players in these institutions wield substantial influence over financial markets and the economy. This concentration of power can be seen in the high salaries and bonuses paid to top executives and traders, as well as in the significant profits generated by these firms.

2. Social and Economic Mobility:

Entry into the upper echelons of the UK's financial sector often requires a specific educational background, typically involving prestigious universities and business schools. While merit and talent play roles, the pathway to these institutions and subsequently to top financial positions can be heavily influenced by socio-economic background. This creates barriers to entry for individuals from less privileged backgrounds, reinforcing the idea of a finance caste.

3. Influence on Policy and Society:

Financial elites in the UK often have substantial influence over economic policy. This influence can be exerted through lobbying efforts, political donations, and direct advisory roles to government officials. The "revolving door" phenomenon, where individuals move between roles in government and the financial sector, further blurs the lines between public policy and private financial interests. This can lead to policies that favor the financial sector at the expense of broader societal needs.

4. Wealth and Inequality:

The disparity in income and wealth between those at the top of the financial sector and the average worker is stark. The concentration of wealth among financial elites contributes to wider economic inequality in the UK. This inequality is often perpetuated across generations, as wealth and the advantages it brings are passed down, entrenching the position of those within the finance caste.

5. Cultural and Social Networks:

The finance caste in the UK is often reinforced by tight-knit social networks. These networks are maintained through elite schools, exclusive clubs, and social events that are not accessible to the general population. This creates an environment where opportunities and information are shared within a closed group, further entrenching their privileged position.

Evidence and Analysis:

Several studies and reports have highlighted the growing influence and power of the financial sector in the UK. For example, the concentration of high-paying jobs and significant bonuses in the City of London has been well-documented. Research has shown that social mobility within the sector is limited, with a disproportionate number of top positions held by individuals from privileged backgrounds.

Moreover, the financial sector's lobbying efforts and influence on policy have been the subject of scrutiny, especially following the 2008 financial crisis. Critics argue that regulatory and policy decisions often favor the interests of the financial sector, sometimes at the expense of broader economic stability and social equity.

In conclusion, the UK does exhibit characteristics of a finance caste, where a distinct and influential group within the financial sector holds significant power, wealth, and influence. This group benefits from a combination of socio-economic barriers, concentrated financial power, and strong influence over public policy, contributing to broader economic inequality and limited social mobility. Understanding this dynamic is crucial for addressing the challenges of inequality and ensuring that economic policies serve the broader population, not just a privileged few.

A Poetry Synopsis

"Does the UK have a Caste System."

In modern streets where freedom sings,

Do hidden layers spread their wings?

A tale of class, a silent thread,

Does caste still linger, though unsaid?

From history's grasp, we've sought to flee,

Yet echoes linger, plain to see.

In accents, schools, and where we dwell,

Do unseen barriers cast their spell?

The old divisions, rich and poor,

Seem softer now, but still endure.

TAI-ZAMARAI YASHARAHYALAH

From titles grand to wealth's embrace,

Do silent lines divide our place?

Opportunity, they say, is free,

Yet doors swing shut for you, not me.

In boardrooms high and factories low,

Does merit rise, or status show?

Though legally, no caste decree,

Does birth still shape our destiny?

In subtle ways, society's mold,

Defines who rises, who is sold.

Through every layer, thick or thin,

We ask if fairness lies within.

Is privilege a silent king,

In the heart of Britain's spring?

So let us question, let us seek,

A world where each voice freely speaks.

Where barriers fade and merit shines,

The Dark Reality of Banking: Understanding the Creation of Money

And true equality defines.

In every heart, in every face,

A chance to grow, a common grace.

Let's break the caste, both old and new,

For justice clear, for all that's true.

TAI-ZAMARAI YASHARAHYALAH

Streams of Poetry

The Dark Reality of Banking: Understanding the Creation of Money

"In the Vaults of Creation."

In the vaults where shadows dance,

Banks weave wealth in a spectral trance.

Through promissory whispers and ledgered dreams,

They craft reality from ethereal streams.

Not mere keepers of golden threads,

But conjurers where the unseen treads.

They mint the future in ink and code,

Sculpting the roads where economies explode.

Yet, in this power lies a frail balance,

A tightrope walk between growth and malice.

For unchecked, their magic breeds despair,

Inflating bubbles in the thin, thin air.

So, let us rewrite the spells they cast,

With wisdom gleaned from errors past.

Let small banks and communities rise,

Grounding finance in honest ties.

For in local hands, trust finds its home,

In every handshake, in every loan.

Thus, stability will grace the land,

From bustling cities to fields of sand.

And as we stand on this threshold bright,

Guardians of wealth must wield their might,

With clarity, purpose, and ethical light,

To forge a future just and right.

The Journey

"The Modern Day Alchemists."

In towers tall where glass gleams cold,

The alchemists of finance mold.

From naught they spin our coins and notes,

With laws that govern unseen votes.

The Dark Reality of Banking: Understanding the Creation of Money

They promise dreams in paper and screen,

Yet tethered are we to what's unseen.

For every loan and ledgered name,

Bears the weight of economic flame.

Missteps in this delicate dance,

Can thrust the world into a trance,

Where bubbles rise on hopes misplaced,

And fortunes crumble, dreams effaced.

But not all is shadowed in this domain,

For light can pierce through greed's own rain.

With regulations firm and just,

We shape a system built on trust.

Small banks, the heart of our renew,

Community's pulse, the tried and true.

They anchor finance to the ground,

In them, a safer world is found.

Thus, we march towards horizons new,

With lessons learned and visions true.

To guard the power banks now hold,

With wisdom, courage, and hearts bold.

The Future

"A Canvas Yet to Be Drawn."

In a realm where digits reign,

Where fortunes shift in a silent chain,

We ponder futures yet to unfold,

In tales of silver and of gold.

The architects of fiscal streams,

Weigh dreams and debts on fragile beams.

Their actions, ripples in a pond,

Shape destinies in realms beyond.

But vision clear and tempered hand,

The Dark Reality of Banking: Understanding the Creation of Money

Can steer us to a promised land.

Where small banks nurture seeds of hope,

And communities find a broader scope.

Through storms of past, we chart our course,

With new frameworks as our guiding force.

A world where finance serves the whole,

With equity and human soul.

Let this be the anthem sung,

In every heart, old and young.

To build a system fair and bright,

In the dawn of economic light.

In these verses, let the essence flow,

Of banking's tale, both high and low.

And in the rhythm of this song,

Let wisdom guide us right from wrong.

TAI-ZAMARAI YASHARAHYALAH

The Symphony of Stability

"Harmony in the Ledger's Lines."

In the corridors of fiscal might,

Where digits dance in the dead of night,

Banks, the conductors of wealth's grand play,

Compose the symphony of our day.

From thin air, they summon gold,

In records where fortunes are bold.

Yet, with each note they choose to write,

Lies the power to uplift or blight.

Through ages past, in shadows deep,

Their secrets lay in vaults to keep.

But now we seek to understand,

The magic wrought by unseen hand.

With prudence, let us tune this art,

The Dark Reality of Banking: Understanding the Creation of Money

Balancing both brain and heart.

For when banks lend with reckless glee,

Inflation rises, storms the sea.

But in the hands of those who care,

Small banks thrive, communities fare.

They anchor wealth in local soil,

And foster growth through honest toil.

So let us draft a future new,

Where every credit, every due,

Is measured by a mindful gaze,

Ensuring balance in all ways.

For in the end, it's not the gold,

But trust and fairness that we hold,

As treasures of a stable land,

Wrought by a just and guiding hand.

In this ode, may wisdom reign,

TAI-ZAMARAI YASHARAHYALAH

And harmony replace the strain.

For banking's tale is ours to steer,

Toward a future bright and clear.

"Balance and Harmony."

In the dance of day and night,

Harmony finds its perfect light.

Between the sun and moon's embrace,

Balance holds a sacred space.

Mountains high and valleys low,

Rivers swift and forests slow.

Nature's symphony, a gentle plea,

To live in peace, in unity.

Life's rhythm, a steady beat,

Where opposites in grace do meet.

Yin and yang, dark and bright,

Balance brings the soul to flight.

□

The Dark Reality of Banking: Understanding the Creation of Money

Amidst the chaos, find the calm,

In every storm, a soothing balm.

Through ebb and flow, through rise and fall,

Harmony embraces all.

In work and rest, a careful blend,

Where passions soar and spirits mend.

Neither excess nor too spare,

But measured steps with thoughtful care.

Heart and mind in concert play,

Guiding choices day by day.

In every task, in every word,

Let balance be our silent chord.

Between the silence and the sound,

In quiet moments, truth is found.

Harmony whispers in the breeze,

A song of unity, of ease.

TAI-ZAMARAI YASHARAHYALAH

Through life's great dance, in every turn,

Lessons of balance we discern.

To give and take, to hold and free,

Is to align with destiny.

Relationships in tender grace,

Where love and respect find their place.

Each voice, a note, each soul, a part,

Of harmony's eternal art.

In nature's arms, in human heart,

Balance plays its timeless part.

A gentle hand, a guiding star,

Reminds us who we truly are.

For in the balance, there is peace,

In harmony, all worries cease.

A world in sync, a life in tune,

Beneath the sun, beneath the moon.

The Dark Reality of Banking: Understanding the Creation of Money

To walk the path with steady gait,

Neither too soon nor yet too late.

With balance as our guiding key,

We find our place in harmony.

So let us strive, in every deed,

To plant the harmony we need.

In every heart, in every land,

May balance blossom, gently stand.

In life's grand symphony, profound,

Balance and harmony resound.

A melody of peace and grace,

To heal the world, to hold its space.

"Spiritual and Ethical Integrity."

In the quiet of the soul's deep night,

A beacon glows, a guiding light.

TAI-ZAMARAI YASHARAHYALAH

Spiritual whispers, soft and clear,

Lead us to paths of truth, held dear.

Beyond the noise, the worldly chase,

Lies a realm of endless grace.

Where hearts align with purpose true,

And virtues bloom in all we do.

Ethics, the compass, moral north,

Directing every action forth.

In choices made, in words we weave,

Our inner truths, we must believe.

Integrity, a sacred flame,

A steadfast star, an honored name.

To walk in light, to stand up tall,

With honesty, we heed the call.

In moments when the world seems gray,

Our spirit shines, lights up the way.

With kindness pure and justice keen,

The Dark Reality of Banking: Understanding the Creation of Money

We craft a world, serene, pristine.

Spiritual depth, a boundless sea,

A source of strength, of clarity.

In every prayer, in every breath,

We seek the sacred, life and death.

Ethical paths, not always straight,

Yet in their midst, our truths await.

To act with love, with duty's might,

Transforms the dark into the light.

From ancient texts to modern thought,

The lessons learned, the battles fought.

Wisdom's timeless, eternal thread,

Guides us in every step we tread.

In daily life, in mundane tasks,

Our spirit's light in actions basks.

Through acts of grace, through deeds of care,

TAI-ZAMARAI YASHARAHYALAH

We show the world our souls laid bare.

For in the core of every heart,

A spark of divine sets us apart.

To live with truth, with honor high,

Is to transcend, to reach the sky.

Spiritual integrity,

An inner peace, a harmony.

Ethical strength, our anchor strong,

Through life's great sea, it steers us on.

In unity of soul and mind,

A deeper purpose we will find.

To live with love, with truth, with grace,

Is to align with time and space.

So let us tread with feet so light,

Upon this earth, both day and night.

With spiritual and ethical might,

We turn the world from wrong to right.

The Dark Reality of Banking: Understanding the Creation of Money

In the tapestry of life we weave,

A legacy of light we leave.

For future generations' sight,

A beacon bright, a guiding light.

"Sustainability and Environmental Stewardship."

In nature's cradle, where life springs,

The earth, our home, a treasure brings.

With verdant hills and azure seas,

A symphony of life, of trees.

Beneath the sky, so vast, so grand,

We walk this earth, we touch the sand.

Yet heed we must, a call so clear,

To care, to guard, to hold it dear.

Sustain the world, our solemn vow,

To heal the earth, to act, to now.

In every breath, in every tree,

TAI-ZAMARAI YASHARAHYALAH

A promise made to keep it free.

From rivers' flow to mountain's crest,

The earth implores us to invest.

In practices both wise and fair,

To show we truly, deeply care.

The air we breathe, the water pure,

Require our hands to heal, secure.

With mindful steps and hearts alight,

We guard the day, protect the night.

Renewable, the way we tread,

With sun and wind, our paths are fed.

A shift from fossil's grim embrace,

To sources bright, to nature's grace.

In every seed, in every bloom,

A chance to stave off pending doom.

Permaculture, a guiding light,

To nurture soil, to set things right.

□

The Dark Reality of Banking: Understanding the Creation of Money

Reduce, reuse, recycle's call,

A mantra shared, embraced by all.

From plastic waste to carbon's trace,

We seek to cleanse, to heal this place.

Sustainability, our creed,

To serve the earth in every deed.

Environmental stewardship,

Our pledge to heal, to not let slip.

To oceans deep and forests vast,

We owe a future, free at last.

From pollution's dark, encroaching blight,

To ecosystems rich and bright.

With wisdom gleaned from ancient lore,

We plant anew, we thus restore.

In balance, harmony, we find,

A future bright for all mankind.

TAI-ZAMARAI YASHARAHYALAH

So let us rise, with voices clear,

To champion what we hold dear.

For in each act of stewardship,

We steer the world on nature's ship.

Together, we can turn the tide,

With love, with care, with planet-wide

Commitment to a greener earth,

A legacy of priceless worth.

In every tree and creature's song,

In nature's realm, we all belong.

To sustain, to guard, to deeply care,

Our earth, our home, our love affair.

"Tech Savvy and Adaptation."

In the dawn of the digital age,

Where screens and codes turn every page,

A world anew, both vast and bright,

The Dark Reality of Banking: Understanding the Creation of Money

Where minds must learn to seek the light.

The heartbeat of our modern time,

In circuits hums and data chimes.

A language built on ones and zeros,

Crafts new paths for future heroes.

To navigate this tech-savvy realm,

Requires a hand upon the helm.

Adapt we must, with eyes that gleam,

To sail upon this digital stream.

The old ways shift, the new ways rise,

In every pixel, truths and lies.

Discern we must, with sharpened mind,

The gold within the data mined.

In apps and tools, a new frontier,

To innovate and persevere.

From AI's reach to blockchain's might,

TAI-ZAMARAI YASHARAHYALAH

We carve new paths in endless night.

With every click, a door swings wide,

To knowledge vast and wonders spied.

Adaptation is the key,

To thrive in this technology.

Embrace the change, the swift, the bold,

In every upgrade, futures unfold.

With curiosity as our guide,

We conquer waves, we turn the tide.

Connections form in virtual space,

A global touch, a shared embrace.

In networks vast, our spirits blend,

In common quests, as hearts extend.

From smart devices in our hands,

To quantum leaps in distant lands,

The pace is swift, the world is wide,

Yet in this flux, we learn, we stride.

The Dark Reality of Banking: Understanding the Creation of Money

Challenges, yes, they surely come,

In every glitch, in every hum.

Yet with resolve, we press ahead,

To future realms, by courage led.

Tech-savvy minds, adapt with grace,

In every byte, a future trace.

With wisdom gleaned from every code,

We pave the paths, we set the mode.

So let us rise, both young and old,

In this brave world, be strong, be bold.

For in this age of tech and change,

Adaptation is our range.

In every challenge, seek the clue,

For growth, for hope, for skies so blue.

Tech-savvy hearts and minds that dare,

To shape the world, to dream, to care.

TAI-ZAMARAI YASHARAHYALAH
"Lifelong Learning and Growth."

In the tapestry of endless time,

Learning's thread, a silver line.

From cradle days to twilight's glow,

A journey vast, where minds must grow.

In youth's embrace, the world is new,

Curiosity's spark, a vivid hue.

Eyes wide open, hearts so pure,

A thirst for knowledge, bright and sure.

As years unfold, the lessons blend,

In every turn, around each bend.

Books and wisdom, mentors wise,

Illuminate our seeking eyes.

Failure's touch, a teacher true,

In every fall, a strength anew.

Resilience builds, as lessons learned,

Through trials faced and triumphs earned.

The Dark Reality of Banking: Understanding the Creation of Money

In every craft, in every art,

Learning's pulse, a beating heart.

From skills refined to insights deep,

The seeds of growth, we always reap.

Embrace the change, the winds of time,

In every challenge, a hill to climb.

Adapt, evolve, in each new phase,

With wisdom's light, we find our ways.

Connections forged in shared pursuits,

Ideas exchanged, in fertile roots.

Communities of thought and dream,

In unity, our spirits gleam.

Technology, a modern sage,

Guides us through this digital age.

With open mind and eager hand,

Explore the vast, uncharted land.

TAI-ZAMARAI YASHARAHYALAH

In moments still, in quiet's grace,

Reflection finds its sacred place.

Meditate on lessons past,

And future paths are clear and vast.

Lifelong learning, a sacred vow,

In every breath, in here and now.

A quest for more, a journey grand,

With open heart, we take our stand.

Growth unbounded, ever true,

In every dawn, in every view.

A life of learning, rich and wide,

With wisdom as our constant guide.

So cherish each and every day,

In knowledge's light, we find our way.

For in the end, what we bestow,

Is a legacy of all we know.

In this endless, boundless quest,

The Dark Reality of Banking: Understanding the Creation of Money

Lies the heart of our life's best.

To learn, to grow, to seek, to find,

The endless riches of the mind.

"Reverbration of 2008: The Banking Crisis."

In towers high, where fortunes grew,

An empire's fall was overdue.

Beneath the gilded, mirrored skies,

The whispers of a storm would rise.

In halls of glass and ivory walls,

The banking giants played with thralls.

With greed unchained and caution tossed,

They gambled much but counted costs.

Mortgages bundled, sliced, and sold,

The alchemy of paper gold.

The markets soared on phantom wings,

TAI-ZAMARAI YASHARAHYALAH

A castle built on fragile things.

Then came the day, the reckoning,

When whispers turned to deafening.

The mighty Lehman's pillars cracked,

A house of cards that tumbled back.

Panic spread like wild fire's breath,

The world awoke to looming death.

Banks too big to fail, or so they said,

Were crumbling, drowning in their dread.

The lifeblood of the global trade,

Now frozen in a grim cascade.

From Wall Street's depths to main street's cries,

The pain was shared in countless lives.

Homes were lost and dreams delayed,

As governments rushed in, dismayed.

With bailouts vast and debtors' plea,

They tried to stem the rolling sea.

The Dark Reality of Banking: Understanding the Creation of Money

In aftermath, the lessons clear,

Of hubris high and unchecked cheer.

Regulation's call grew strong,

To right the path where it went wrong.

Yet echoes of that fateful year,

Still linger in our hearts, unclear.

For in the dance of finance bright,

The shadows lurk in gold's soft light.

May we remember, ever more,

The crisis of two thousand and eight's roar.

To guard against the prideful fall,

And heed the warning to us all.

Acknowledgements

I am deeply grateful to my beloved sons, Abiyah Shalah Yasharahyalah, Tai-Zamarai Yasharahyalah (Junior) and Barak (Chazahrayah). Your unwavering love, boundless curiosity, and endless laughter inspire me every rise. You are my greatest joys and my constant reminders of the beauty and wonder in our world.

To my cherished eternal partner, Naiyahmi Yasharahyalah, your unwavering support, understanding, and encouragement have been my guiding light through every step of this journey. Your belief in me has fuelled my determination and given me the strength to persevere in the face of challenges. Thank you for being my rock, my confidant, and my most cherished companion.

The Dark Reality of Banking: Understanding the Creation of Money

I extend my heartfelt appreciation to my family and friends who have stood by me with love, patience, and encouragement throughout the writing process. Your words of encouragement, listening ears, and shared laughter have been invaluable to me.

To my mentors, colleagues, and collaborators, thank you for sharing your wisdom, insights, and expertise. Your guidance and support have enriched my understanding and fueled my passion for the topics explored in this book.

I am grateful to the readers who have embraced my work with open minds and open hearts. Your curiosity, feedback, and engagement inspire me to continue learning, growing, and sharing my knowledge with the world.

Lastly, I express my profound gratitude to the countless individuals whose teachings, stories, and experiences have shaped the content of this book. Your voices echo through these pages, reminding us all of the interconnectedness of our journeys and the boundless potential within each of us.

To my sons, partner, family, friends, mentors, collaborators, readers, and all those who have touched my life in ways big and small, I offer my deepest thanks. Your presence in my life is a gift beyond measure, and I am honoured to share this journey with you.

TAI-ZAMARAI YASHARAHYALAH

About the Author

Tai-Zamarai Yasharahyalah stands out as a distinguished figure in the realm of economic thought and financial systems, blending a deep understanding of economics with a profound appreciation for the interconnectedness of human society and the natural world. Rooted in the rich traditions of the Ibar (Indigenous Ancient Hebrew) cultural heritage, Tai-Zamarai's perspective on economics is enriched by a holistic worldview that honors the wisdom of ancestral knowledge and the rhythms of nature.

Tai-Zamarai's journey in the field of economics is marked by a unique blend of scholarly rigor and spiritual insight. With an academic background in Medical Genetics from Queen Mary's University of London, Tai-Zamarai possesses a solid foundation in scientific inquiry, which he seamlessly integrates with his passion for exploring the intricate dynamics of financial systems and their impact on human well-being.

☐

The Dark Reality of Banking: Understanding the Creation of Money

Beyond his academic achievements, Tai-Zamarai is a certified Life Coach accredited by the International Coach Federation (ICF) and an expert in Plant-Based Nutrition. These credentials underscore his commitment to promoting holistic well-being, not only through financial literacy but also through conscious living and mindful nourishment.

In *The Dark Reality of Banking: Understanding the Creation of Money*, Tai-Zamarai unveils the hidden mechanisms of the banking system, challenging conventional perceptions and revealing the profound implications of money creation on the economy and individual lives. His exploration goes beyond mere financial analysis, delving into the psychological and emotional impacts of financial anxiety and the societal narratives that shape our understanding of value and scarcity.

Tai-Zamarai's unique approach bridges the gap between economics and spirituality, offering readers a transformative perspective on financial systems and their role in shaping human consciousness and societal structures. With a masterful blend of empirical evidence and poetic expression, he invites readers to embark on a journey of self-discovery and enlightenment, uncovering the deeper truths behind the façade of modern banking.

Join Tai-Zamarai Yasharahyalah on a profound exploration of economic reality and spiritual awakening, and discover how a deeper understanding of money creation can lead to a more harmonious and equitable world. His work is a call to rethink the foundations of our financial systems and to embrace a holistic approach to economic well-being and personal fulfillment.

Glossary of Key Terms

Asset Bubble: A situation in which the price of assets rises significantly over their intrinsic value, often driven by speculative demand.

Cognitive-Behavioral Strategies: Techniques used to change patterns of thinking or behavior that are causing people's problems, and thus change the way they feel.

Community Lending: Financial practices that involve local banks or credit unions providing loans to individuals or businesses within a community to foster local economic growth.

Credit Guidance: Policies or strategies aimed at directing credit to productive sectors of the economy to support sustainable growth.

Debt Management: Strategies and practices for handling and repaying debt in a manageable and responsible manner.

Emergency Fund: Savings set aside to cover unexpected expenses or financial emergencies.

Environmental, Social, and Governance (ESG) Criteria: Standards for a company's operations that socially conscious investors use to screen potential investments.

Financial Anxiety: Worry or stress related to financial matters, such as debt, expenses, and economic security.

Fractional Reserve Banking: A banking system in which only a fraction of bank deposits is backed by actual cash on hand and available for withdrawal.

Holistic Well-being: An approach to health that considers the whole person and how he or she interacts with the environment, emphasizing the connection of mind, body, and spirit.

Inflation: The rate at which the general level of prices for goods and services rises, leading to a decrease in purchasing power.

Minimalism: A lifestyle that emphasizes simplicity and reducing excess, focusing on what is essential and meaningful.

Mindfulness: A mental state achieved by focusing one's awareness on the present moment, while calmly acknowledging and accepting one's feelings, thoughts, and bodily sensations.

Promissory Note: A financial instrument containing a written promise by one party to pay another party a definite sum of money either on demand or at a specified future date.

Regulatory Framework: A set of regulations and guidelines developed by authorities to oversee and control the operations of financial institutions.

Sustainability: The ability to maintain or improve standards of living without damaging or depleting natural resources for future generations.

Systemic Risk: The risk of collapse of an entire financial system or entire market, due to the potential failure of a single entity or group of entities.

The Dark Reality of Banking: Understanding the Creation of Money

Additional Resources and References

Books:

1. *Debt: The First 5,000 Years* by David Graeber

2. *The End of Alchemy: Money, Banking, and the Future of the Global Economy* by Mervyn King

3. *Other People's Money: The Real Business of Finance* by John Kay

Articles:

1. *"How Do Banks Create Money and Why Can Other Firms Not Do the Same?"* – Richard A. Werner

2. *"The Truth About Banks"* – The Economist

Websites:

1. *[The Financial Times](https://www.ft.com)* - For current financial news and analysis.

2. *[Investopedia](https://www.investopedia.com)* - For definitions and explanations of financial terms and concepts.

3. *[Bank of England](https://www.bankofengland.co.uk)* - For insights and publications on monetary policy and financial stability.

Reports:

1. *"Money Creation in the Modern Economy"* – Bank of England Quarterly Bulletin 2014 Q1

2. *"The Future of Banking"* – World Economic Forum

The Dark Reality of Banking: Understanding the Creation of Money

Educational Programs:

1. Financial Literacy Courses – Available through various online platforms such as Coursera and Khan Academy.

2. Community College Financial Planning Programs – Offering practical education on managing personal finances.

Teaser Poetry

1. Perception's Dance

In the realm where thoughts entwine,

Reality and dreams combine.

A wisp of fear, a thread of hope,

In this web, we learn to cope.

2. Beyond the Illusion

Scarcity, a ghostly veil,

In abundance, we prevail.

Value found in heart and mind,

In simplicity, we find.

3. Harmony's Call

In balance, life's true essence lies,

Where health and wealth harmonize.

A path where values intertwine,

The Dark Reality of Banking: Understanding the Creation of Money

In this journey, light will shine.

4. Reverb of the Past

2008's shadow, a lesson clear,

In crisis, we confront our fear.

Regulations, new paths forge,

In wisdom, our strength will surge.

5. Future's Light

Tech and truth, in tandem grow,

Adapt, evolve, and let it show.

Sustain the earth, and spirit too,

In this future, dreams come true.

Thanks for reading! Please add a short review on Amazon and let me know what you thought!

www.ingramcontent.com/pod-product-compliance
Lightning Source LLC
Chambersburg PA
CBHW071911210526
45479CB00002B/376